Fodor's
25 Best

KRAKOW

How to Use This Book

KEY TO SYMBOLS

✚	Map reference to the accompanying fold-out map	🚢	Nearest riverboat or ferry stop
✉	Address	♿	Facilities for visitors with disabilities
☎	Telephone number	❓	Other practical information
🕐	Opening/closing times	▷	Further information
🍴	Restaurant or café	ℹ	Tourist information
🚆	Nearest rail station	✋	Admission charges: Expensive (over 35PLN/€10), Moderate (10–35PLN/€3–€10) and Inexpensive (under 10PLN/€3)
Ⓜ	Nearest Metro (subway) station		
🚌	Nearest bus route		

This guide is divided into four sections

• Essential Krakow: An introduction to the city and tips on making the most of your stay.

• Krakow by Area: We've broken the city into six areas, and recommended the best sights, shops, entertainment venues, nightlife and restaurants in each one. Suggested walks help you to explore on foot.

• Where to Stay: The best hotels, whether you're looking for luxury, budget or something in between.

• Need to Know: The info you need to make your trip run smoothly, including getting about by public transport, weather tips, emergency phone numbers and useful websites.

Navigation In the Krakow by Area chapter, we've given each area its own color, which is also used on the locator maps throughout the book and the map on the inside front cover.

Maps The fold-out map accompanying this book is a comprehensive street plan of Krakow. The grid on this fold-out map is the same as the grid on the locator maps within the book. We've given grid references within the book for each sight and listing.

Contents

Introducing Krakow

Krakow has a great tradition of hospitality, and has been welcoming visitors since the medieval period. Its old buildings are beautifully restored, yet as a university city it has moved with the times, kept young and vibrant by its lively student population.

There's more than one Krakow to experience and you can see many different faces of the city in a day, since it's an easy place to negotiate. Its attractions are concentrated in the relatively small area of the Old Town, whose streets have barely changed since they were laid out in the 13th century. It's all walkable, but be prepared for lots of stairs. Cafés, restaurants, bars and clubs occupy every corner and floor, from the cellars to the attics to the courtyards. It's one of the thrills of Krakow life to push open an ancient wooden door and hear the very latest band pulsing up from below. But if you prefer your music more gentle, you can sit beneath a 17th-century stucco ceiling or in a magnificent baroque church to hear the work of a great composer.

Maybe you just want to have a straightforward good time in the Old Town. No problem—you'll find accommodation, food and entertainment that's reasonably priced by Western European standards, and English is widely understood. Yet, while tourism is important to Krakow, the city has in no way surrendered its own identity to it. As a former capital of Poland—a country that has been invaded time and again and come back fighting, sometimes after centuries of foreign occupation—it is fiercely proud of its traditions.

The latest area to revive is Kazimierz, the former Jewish district. Its people were annihilated in World War II, yet their culture is again being celebrated. Spend the evening listening to *klezmer* music or sitting in one of Kazimierz's bars.

You don't have to go to any museums or art galleries—though Krakow has many—to absorb the soul of this very varied city.

FACTS AND FIGURES

- Population: 755,000.
- Size of Rynek Główny: 210m x 212m (229 x 231 yards), the largest medieval square in Europe.
- Number of churches: 119.
- Number of bars: 400-plus in the Old Town alone.

MERCHANT CITY

Krakow's early wealth came from its location on the main trade routes between Europe and Asia, and the Baltic and the Mediterranean. Then, as now, it was a cosmopolitan city. The salt mined nearby at Wieliczka and Bochnia made Krakow's grand families rich and paid for its beautiful buildings.

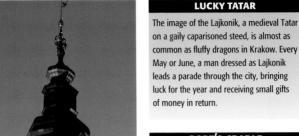

LUCKY TATAR

The image of the Lajkonik, a medieval Tatar on a gaily caparisoned steed, is almost as common as fluffy dragons in Krakow. Every May or June, a man dressed as Lajkonik leads a parade through the city, bringing luck for the year and receiving small gifts of money in return.

POPE'S CRADLE

Krakow is the city that raised the first Polish pope. Karol Wojtyła lived here as a student of literature, worker, actor, poet and priest. As bishop and archbishop, he was the students' favorite; as John Paul II he drew hundreds of thousands of Poles to celebrate Mass on Krakow's Błonia fields.

A Short Stay in Krakow

DAY 1

Morning Breakfast in one of the cafés in Rynek Główny—Main Square—and you'll see some of the best city sights from your table.

Mid-morning Walk up the Royal Route of ul. Grodska to **Wawel Hill** (▷ 62–67) and the Cathedral where the kings of Poland and some of its heroes are laid to rest, then tour the Castle. After taking in the view over the Vistula River toward the futuristic **Manggha Japanese Center** (▷ 95), make your way down to the riverside **Dragon's Lair** (▷ 66) and get close to the Smok, who breathes real fire.

Lunch In summer, eat on one of the floating restaurants moored here or cook your own Polish sausage at an open-air barbecue restaurant. In winter, make you way back to ul. św. Anny and the popular **Chimera Salad Bar** (▷ 58).

Afternoon Back in the Rynek Główny, **St. Mary's Church** (▷ 26–27) is a must-see, after which you can examine the fine facades of the **Kamienice** (▷ 25), the noblemen's houses that line the square. If you have the energy, finish in the **Sukiennice** (▷ 30–31) in the center of the square, whose stalls sell every kind of souvenir.

Dinner In a city that has welcomed visitors for centuries, one restaurant takes the prize. Eat at **Wierzynek** (▷ 29, 38), which has been feeding guests since 1364 and has a fine view of the square and the little church of **St. Adalbert's** (▷ 33).

Evening If you're a clubber, make for **Prozak** (▷ 57) or the less sophisticated **Jazz Rock Café** (▷ 57). Quieter souls can take in a film at **Cracow Cinema Center Ars** (▷ 57) or just have a nightcap.

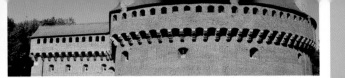

DAY 2

Morning Take a stroll in the Planty before breakfast and see students rushing to their lectures—beware of cyclists. Wherever your stroll finishes, turn in toward the center of town for breakfast and you'll find a choice of atmospheric cafés in the side streets.

Mid-morning You have a date with a lady—but she belongs to Leonardo. In the **Czartoryski Palace Museum** (▷ 46–47), you can see da Vinci's *Lady with an Ermine* and a host of other treasures.

Lunch Try something typically Polish, among some typical Poles, at an old-fashioned "milk bar," an inexpensive self-service café that would originally just have served up glasses of milk but now offers traditional home-cooked dishes. Tiny **U Stasi** (▷ 58) is as good a choice as any.

Afternoon Work off your meal with a 20-minute walk to Kazimierz, the former Jewish quarter. Or be lazy and take a tram. Start at plac Wolnica by visiting the **Ethnographic Museum** (▷ 72–73) before exploring the synagogues, or walk down ul. Miodowa to ul. Szeroka, the hub of most of the Jewish restaurants and historic buildings.

Dinner After maybe browsing for books or antiques or dropping in on a lecture at the **Galicia Jewish Museum** (▷ 77), shake off the seriousness at one of the many restaurants that features *klezmer* music. They serve a nostalgic kind of Jewish cuisine to accompany the uplifting tunes.

Evening The night is always young in Kazimierz. Begin a café crawl at **Alchemia** (▷ 83)—there may be a good band on at its adjoining Music Hall. Then continue around **Plac Nowy** (▷ 74) and the streets leading off it, according to taste.

Top 25

▶ ▶ ▶

Jama Michalika ▷ 44
This café was the haunt of Krakow's artistic society at the turn of the 20th century.

Kamienice ▷ 25 These grand noblemen's houses in the Old Town give Krakow its medieval character.

Katedra Wawelska ▷ 62–63 Wawel Cathedral is the country's most important church.

Kopalnia Soli Wieliczka ▷ 102–103 Wieliczka Salt Mine has jaw-dropping underground caverns.

Kościół Franciszkanów ▷ 45 The Franciscan Church is noted for its beautiful stained glass.

Kościół Mariacki ▷ 26–27 St. Mary's Church is a Gothic masterpiece.

Muzeum Dom Mehoffera ▷ 88–89 Mehoffer's House was home to one of Krakow's leading artists.

Muzeum Etnograficzne ▷ 72–73 The city's Ethnographic Museum.

Muzeum Książąt Czartoryskich ▷ 46–47 Da Vinci's *Lady with an Ermine* resides here.

Muzeum Narodowe w Krakowie ▷ 90–91 The National Museum is the place to find out about Polish modern art.

Pałac Królewski na Wawelu ▷ 64–65 Wawel Castle was the seat of Poland's kings for centuries.

Pałac Biskupa Ezrama Ciołka ▷ 49 This palace houses the Museum of Art of Old Poland.

Muzeum Wyspiańskiego ▷ 48 The Wyspiański Museum celebrates the Krakow-born artist.

Shopping

The wealth created by the salt mines meant that from the earliest times, Krakow's gentry could afford to buy silks from the East and import art and architects from Italy. Today, much of the trade comes from tourism, yet so far Krakow has resisted the usual mass-produced souvenirs (the stalls at the Dragon's Cave excepted) and you are more likely to bring home some kind of locally produced craftwork.

Amber

Bursztyń, in Polish, is everywhere in Poland and the Baltic states and Krakow is no exception. Since it consists of the solidified resin of prehistoric pine trees, it is not as hard as some gemstones and it feels warm against the skin. Most of the amber you will see on sale is an opaque honey-yellow or a transparent tea color. Sometimes an insect or small fern, trapped in the amber as it solidified, forms an intrinsic part of the design. Always check that you are buying genuine amber. Some of the inexpensive pendants on sale in souvenir shops will be plastic. Do not buy for investment unless you are an expert.

Jewelry

Poland has a strong design tradition and this is particularly true of the jewelry you'll see on sale in the Old Town. Usually in silver with gemstones or amber but often in acrylic, too, pieces make a unique memento.

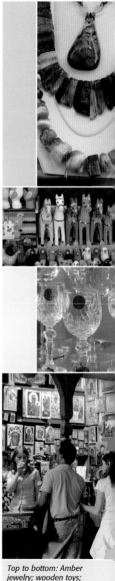

Top to bottom: Amber jewelry; wooden toys; crystal glasses; a stall in the Cloth Hall

---

SHOPPING MALLS

If you are suffering withdrawal symptoms from the big-city shopping experience, Krakow now has plenty of places to spend your złoty. Packed with international retail chains, Galeria Krakowska stands conveniently next to the railway station and is the city's most accessible mall. If you are willing to travel farther afield, Krakow Plaza is a short bus and tram ride east along aleja Pokoju, while Galeria Kazimierz lies to the southeast of the Old Town on ul. Podgórska.

Food and Drink

You'll find many varieties of vodka on sale
(▷ 13). Not quite so strong is *miód pitny*,
a kind of mead. Polish chocolates are a little
different from their Western European and
American counterparts. See a good range in
Wawel or Wedel, both in the Rynek Główny.
Plums and praline are popular fillings.

Arts and Crafts

You can buy wooden trinket boxes and carved
wooden items, usually in a naïve style that
is typical of the countryside around Krakow.
Small stained-glass hangings are pretty. Some
of the embroidered blouses that are part of
the regional folk garb are wearable without the
rest of the costume, and linen tablecloths and
napkins are good value. You'll find an excellent selection of leather goods, particularly
bags, which are usually more serviceable than
designer. Also very practical are sheepskin
gloves and slippers. Something you don't find in
many other places is armor. You'll see swords,
chainmail and helmets all on sale, of varying
degrees of authenticity.

Christmas Market

Stalls crowd the main square for the month of
December, and mulled wine and grilled snacks
are on sale to help you get in the mood to buy.
Mostly the goods are similar to what's available
year-round, but with the emphasis on gifts. The
Christmas Market is one of the most magical
experiences in Krakow, especially in the snow.

*Top to bottom: Flavored
vodka; fashionable
clothing; handmade lace;
jars of pickles*

STREET EATS

Every street in Krakow's Old Town seems to have a stall
or two selling *obwarzanki*—tasty pretzels sprinkled with
poppy seeds or sesame seeds, and ideal to nibble with a
beer in the sunshine. You'll also see the sellers of *oscypek*,
with baskets of this squeaky, usually smoked, sheeps'
milk cheese, traditionally made in the Tatra Mountains.
In winter, it's grilled over braziers and sold hot during the
Christmas market.

Shopping by Theme

Small shops with a strong, individual character are still common in Krakow, but you'll find your favorite labels are well represented too, especially in the big shopping centers just outside the old town. For more details, see the listings in Krakow by Area.

Antiques/Curios
Antyki Józefa (▷ 82)
Galeria Osobliwości
 (▷ 56)
Galeria Rycerska (▷ 56)
Galeria Szalom (▷ 82)

Arts and Crafts
Dekor Art (▷ 56)
Galeria Olympia (▷ 82)
Galerie D'Art Naïf (▷ 82)
Indalo Café (▷ 96)

Books and Media
Austeria (▷ 82)
Cracow Poster Gallery
 (▷ 56)
Galicia Jewish Museum
 (▷ 77)
High Synagogue (▷ 79)
Księgarnia Camena
 (▷ 36)

Clothing
Click (▷ 56)
Zebra (▷ 36)

Food and Drink
Ciasteczka z Krakowa
 (▷ 56)
Delicatesy (▷ 36)
Krakowski Kredens
 (▷ 56)
Produkty Benedyktyńskie
 (▷ 82)
Szambelan (▷ 36)
Wawel (▷ 36)

Glass
Alhena (▷ 36)
Polskie Szkło (▷ 56)

Jewelry
Blazko Kindery (▷ 82)
Diament (▷ 56)
Galeria Ora (▷ 56)

Malls
Galeria Kazimierz (▷ 82)
Pasaż 13 (▷ 36)

Markets
Plac Nowy (▷ 74,
 panel, 82)
Stary Kleparz (▷ panel,
 96)

Souvenirs/Gifts
Lu'lua (▷ 82)
Sukiennice (▷ 36)

Krakow by Night

Despite the vast range and number of bars in the Old Town, Krakow nightlife is not only about drinking. As a student city, Krakow has its share of clubs, but film is very popular here too, with many cinemas showing movies in the original language. Music of every contemporary genre pulses through the cellars in the Old Town, while lovers of classical music can enjoy many beautiful venues.

Relaxed Summers

In summer, most cafés, bars and restaurants have outside tables and the fine buildings in the Old Town are dramatically lit at night. Rynek Główny is filled with diners and drinkers, and the lack of traffic, apart from the occasional horse-drawn carriage, means you can hear the buzz of conversation. In general, it's safe to wander within the Planty in the evenings. Kazimierz is a little more edgy but things are generally good-humored and peaceful.

Winter Retreats

When winter arrives, the cellar bars and thick stone walls of the venerable buildings really come into their own. Doors are kept closed to hold the heat in, so push at that 14th-century plank of wood studded with iron and you may find a restaurant with a roaring fire or a jazz band working up a sweat. No one wants to venture back out into the cold, which may be how the Krakow tradition of staying open "until the last guest" began.

VODKA LORE

Learning about vodka can be an entertainment in itself, and bar staff will be happy to teach you. Usually distilled from rye and widely accepted as the world's purest, Polish vodka comes in various flavors, but until you see a Krakow bar you may not have appreciated quite how many. Żubrówka, or bison-grass vodka, and cherry-flavored Wiśniówka are two of the most common. Wyborowa, which means exquisite, is a good brand.

Top to bottom: A jazz concert; juggling fire; a Polish band on stage; a jazz club; a hot-air balloon on Rynek Główny

Eating Out

The stereotype of Polish food is dumplings and sausage, and it's true that you may be offered well-seasoned lard for your bread rather than butter. But Krakow is now full of excellent restaurants serving lighter dishes from locally farmed ingredients, which disprove the old travelers' tales.

When to Eat
In Krakow, each establishment makes its own rules. The smarter and more ambitious restaurants will keep normal restaurant hours, opening for lunch and dinner only. Most of the other places begin serving by 9am, with some cafés starting as early as 7am, and will stay open until the small hours.

Where to Eat
Some cake shops also serve savory snacks and sandwiches. Some cafés serve only tea, coffee and their home-cooked cheesecake; others serve wine and beer but not vodka and have a more extensive menu of snacks. Nearly all bars will have some kind of sandwich or other snack to help line your stomach, while some of the more atmospheric cellar bars have restaurant areas. In summer, tables spill onto the streets and many places open a secret garden—look for the sign *ogród*—which can be anything from a delightful tree-shaded former monastery plot to the inner courtyard of a grand town house, overhung by upstairs balconies. You'll find the greatest concentration of cafés and restaurants in the Old Town within the Planty and in Kazimierz.

TIPPING

Drink and meal prices are still pretty reasonable by European standards, so tipping is not a painful process. Leaving your bartender some change and rounding up the bill in restaurants to the nearest 5 złoty is common practice (forget 10 percent—most waiters would be shocked to receive so much on top of the bill here). Many serving staff are students who are glad of a little extra money.

Top to bottom: Alchemia bar; Chimera is a cellar restaurant; a pavement café; Chimera Salad Bar

Restaurants by Cuisine

Restaurants in Krakow offer food from around the world for deep and shallow pockets. For a more detailed description of each restaurant, see Krakow by Area.

Top Tips For...

These great suggestions will help you tailor your ideal visit to Krakow, no matter how you choose to spend your time. Each sight or listing has a fuller write-up elsewhere in the book.

KEEPING YOUR CHILDREN HAPPY

Krakow Zoo (▷ 106), in the middle of Las Wolski, has big-cat breeding programs.
The Park Jordana (▷ 94) children's playground is next to Błonia fields.

A WALK IN THE PARK

Stroll in the Botanic Gardens (▷ 95). If wet, there are greenhouses to explore.
Błonia fields (▷ 94) has enough space for everyone in Krakow, including you and your kite.
Greening the city in summer, and giving breathing space in winter, the Planty (▷ 55) is a park for all seasons.

HISTORY'S DARK SIDE

Ulica Pomorska (▷ 95), a museum of Krakow during World War II, is in a former Gestapo building.
The memorial museums at Auschwitz-Birkenau (▷ 100–101) are a powerful reminder of the horrors of the Holocaust.
A simple cross commemorates the murder of thousands of Polish officers at Katyń (▷ 52).

CLASSICAL MUSIC

Within the exuberantly decorated Teatr Słowackiego (▷ 54) you can see visiting artists and companies as well as homegrown opera.
Poland's biggest philharmonic orchestra, the Filharmonia (▷ 57), is joined by the best international musicians.
Many of Krakow's churches, such as SS. Peter and Paul (▷ 52), host regular performances in beautiful surroundings.

Krakow Zoo (above); the r (below)

Teatr Słowackie (below)

A jazz performance (below)

DANCING AT NIGHT

Hedonists shake it all about until the early hours every night at Jazz Rock Café (▷ 57).
Always wanted to shimmy with Lenin? Pub Propaganda (▷ 83) is the place.
Get your glad rags on if you want to join the beautiful people at Prozak (▷ 57).

ALL THAT JAZZ

The cellar of the intimate Harris Piano Bar (▷ 37) is usually crammed full of aficionados.
Spreading out to various venues from the Piwnica Pod Baranami (▷ 33), the July festival is the highspot of the year.
Alchemia's Music Hall (▷ 83) off the main bar hosts jazz concerts with international stars.

TAKING THE LONG VIEW

The old, imposing fort of the Barbakan, just inside the northern edge of the Planty, offers fine views from its upper galleries (▷ 50).
Bring a złoty to look through the telescopes when you get to the top of the Town Hall Tower (▷ 34).
A short hike or bus and tram ride out of the city will bring you to the view from Kościuszko Mound (▷ 104).

Riverside views (above)

ARCHITECTURE OLD AND NEW

The uncompromisingly modern Manggha Japanese Center (▷ 95) provides an antidote to Krakow Gothic.
St. Adalbert's (▷ 33) in the Rynek Główny is one of the city's oldest and smallest churches.
The fin-de-siècle flourishes of the Teatr Słowackiego (▷ 54) were influenced by the Paris Opera.

St. Adalbert's church

STAYING ON A SHOESTRING

Piano Guest House (▷ 109) is a simple but comfortable home from home near the main rail station.

Cybulskiego Guest Rooms (▷ 109) offer mini apartments just outside the Planty.

Café society (above); Hotel Copernicus (below)

CAFÉ SOCIETY

If you've forgotten to bring a book, you can read the walls at Café Larousse (▷ 58).

Singer (▷ 83) started the Kazimierz craze for tables made out of old sewing machines and lots of lace doilies.

Pen and post a verse at Café Gołębia (▷ 58), the *rynna poetycka* or "gutter of poetry."

St. Andrew's (below

SLEEPING IN THE LAP OF LUXURY

You can count the stars from the rooftop rooms at the Hotel Copernicus (▷ 112).

Or count the Tsars who have stayed at the Pod Różą (▷ 112) hotel—Alexander I was one.

For boutique chic, sleep in the history-rich Hotel Maltański (▷ 112).

HISTORIC CHURCHES

The twin towers of the Romanesque St. Andrew's (▷ 51) withstood the Tatar invasion of 1241.

But the unfortunate bugler (▷ 24) in the tower of St. Mary's Church was caught by a Tatar's arrow.

Wawel Cathedral (▷ 62–63) has been the setting for almost all Polish coronations.

JEWISH CULTURE

Visit the Galicia Jewish Museum (▷ 77) to find out how the heritage continues.

Dine at Klezmer-Hois (▷ 84) to hear some of the best *klezmer* bands.

Music at Klezmer-Hois (above right); detail of the altar at St. Mary's Church (right)

Krakow by Area

Laid out in 1257 and the largest in medieval Europe, Krakow's main market square is where everyone meets to relax, buy flowers, celebrate or protest. From 1320, when citizens first paid homage to the king here, it has been at the heart of city life.

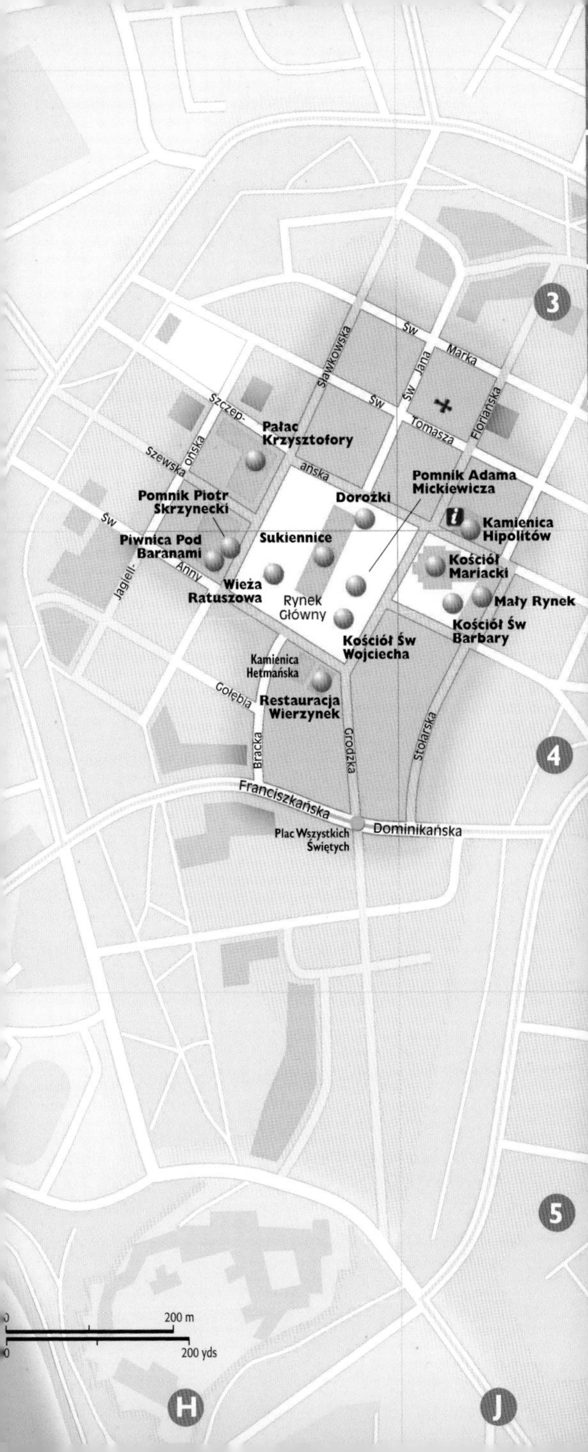

Szczep-

Szewska

Sławkowska

Św

Św Jana

Św Marka

Floriańska

Pałac Krzysztofory

anska

Św Tomasza

Pomnik Adama Mickiewicza

Pomnik Piotr Skrzynecki

Dorożki

Św

Anny

Piwnica Pod Baranami

Sukiennice

Wieża Ratuszowa

Rynek Główny

Kamienica Hipolitów

Kościół Mariacki

Mały Rynek

Kościół Św Barbary

Kościół Św Wojciecha

Jagiell-

Kamienica Hetmańska

Gołębia

Restauracja Wierzynek

Bracka

Grodzka

Stolarska

Franciszkańska

Dominikańska

Plac Wszystkich Świętych

3

4

5

Rynek Główny

200 m

200 yds

H

J

Hejnał

TOP **25**

The bugle call (left); St. Mary's tallest tower (right)

THE BASICS

➕ J4

✉ Kościół Mariacki, may be seen and heard anywhere in and around Rynek Główny

🕐 Hourly day and night, just after the clock chimes the hour. Tower visits 3 May–Sep Tue, Thu, Sat 9–11.30, 1–5.30

♿ None

💷 Free to listen in square; tower visits inexpensive, free on 1 May 12.10–3.30, and 2 May 9–11.30, 1–5.30

HIGHLIGHTS

● View of Barbican and St. Florian's Gate
● View in the opposite direction of Wawel Hill
● For a nominal sum the bugler will pose for a picture with you and give you his autograph and a stamp certifying that you climbed the tower

In a city of wonderful sights, it's strange that the most potent symbol is not seen but heard. The *hejnał*, or bugle call, has sounded from the top of the tallest tower of St. Mary's Church across Krakow's skyline for centuries, and continues to do so today, every hour, round the clock.

The legend The origin of the *hejnał* lies in an era when Krakow was under constant threat of Tatar invasion. One night in 1240, the sentry in St. Mary's Watchtower saw Tatar horsemen approaching just before dawn and sounded his bugle to rouse the troops and citizens. A Tatar arrow caught him in the throat, cutting short his bugle call. Though the sentry was killed, the citizenry had sufficient warning to fight off the invaders and save the city. The sentry was buried with great honor, and down the centuries his bugle call has continued to be played, with the final note cut short in his memory.

Climb the tower Today, the bugler is a member of the modern-day descendants of the watchmen, the fire brigade. In summer, you can climb the 239 steep steps to the little room 54m (177ft) above the ground, where, if you time it right (you won't be allowed to hang around indefinitely, it gets very crowded up there), you can see the bugler in action. The *hejnał* has become a symbol of Poland and is relayed on Polish radio to mark the hour. If you can't climb the tower, do wave when you hear the *hejnał*—the bugler usually waves back.

The Madonna and Child on the facade of a house (left); detail on Bonerowski House (right)

Kamienice

You'll see noblemen's town houses dating back more than 750 years throughout the Old Town but the market square is an ideal place to appreciate them—you don't even have to leave your café table to do so.

Location, location Krakow's Old Town was built following the Tatar invasions that devastated cities all over Poland. In 1257, a charter was granted and the city was laid out according to a regular plan whose streets and squares you still stroll around today. Ownership was strictly defined and all residents, already a multicultural bunch owing to Krakow's position as a crossroads of European trade, were deemed equal under the rule of the local authorities.

Grand designs The houses—and especially their frontages—have changed over the centuries, being remodeled after fires, and in line with fashion and their owners' fortunes. Gothic gave way to Renaissance and baroque style as Italian architects were called in to make them into palaces. One or two of the houses are now museums and many contain restaurants, shops or bars, so you can easily enter to see beautiful details such as vaulted and decorated ceilings. The custom of marking each house with a sign above the door has persisted (*pod* means "under the sign of"). With competing modern shop signs and continuing renovations you are unlikely to spot all the signs on one tour, but keep looking and you'll collect a fair few.

THE BASICS

✠ H4
✉ Rynek Główny
☎ None
🕐 Daily 24 hours
🍴 Many and various (€–€€€)
♿ The square is cobbled but otherwise flat; few shops have ramps
✋ Free

HIGHLIGHTS

● Restored ceilings in the restaurant at Kamienica Szara (No. 6)
● Gothic fighting lizards over the door at Kamienica Pod Jaszczurami (No. 8)
● Wierzynek restaurant in Kamienica Morsztynowska (No. 16)
● 18th-century Virgin painted on the facade of Kamienica Pod Obrazem (No. 19)
● The white eagle on Kamienica Pod Orłem (No. 45)

Kościół Mariacki

HIGHLIGHTS

● Veit Stoss's High Altar
● Slack Crucifix with a figure of Jesus carved from one piece of stone by Veit Stoss
● Silver altar of St. Joseph
● Biblical carvings on choir stalls
● 1890s murals by Jan Matejko
● Great West Window with stone tracery by Matejko, stained glass by Mehoffer and Wyspiański

DID YOU KNOW?

● So lifelike is Veit Stoss's carving that in the 1930s a Krakow professor used it to study medieval skin diseases.
● It's said that Półzygmunt, one of St. Mary's five bells, was carried up the tower in 1438 by one man, Stanisław Ciołek.

If you see one church in Krakow it should be St. Mary's, a Gothic masterpiece: Its two mismatched towers built by rival brothers dominate the city skyline and its interior is crammed with world-class carvings.

City symbol From all over the city you can see St. Mary's two towers, the shorter bell tower topped with a baroque cupola, and the spire of the taller Watchtower encircled by a gold crown. The church entrance between these is for worshipers only; other vistors enter through a side door in Plac Mariacki.

Brick beauty St. Mary's basilica was built between the end of the 13th century and the beginning of the 15th, though the towers and side chapels were not finished until much later,

Clockwise from far left: Detail of the Virgin Mary dying on Veit Stoss's altar; the Jan Sobieski plaque; the High Altar and stained-glass windows; the church's Gothic towers; the High Altar

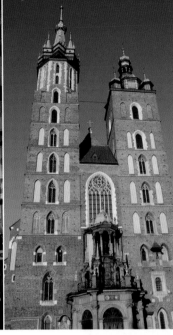

and some of the additions made by artists of the Young Poland movement date from about a century ago. There are also several Renaissance tombs made by Italian artists.

High altar The rich colors and carving inside the basilica can make it difficult to pick out what to look at, but you should focus on the High Altar. Carved between 1477 and 1489 by the best sculptor of the day, Veit Stoss, known as the Master of Nuremburg, it is the largest altar of its kind in Europe. For his work, Veit Stoss was paid the equivalent of the city's budget for a whole year. In several folding sections, the oak and lime-wood altar, measuring 11m (36ft) by almost 13m (42ft), is adorned with around 200 gilded and painted figures, mostly relating to the life of the Virgin Mary—but the faces are people of Krakow who Stoss met in daily life.

THE BASICS

www.mariacki.com

✚ J4

✉ Plac Mariacki 5

☎ 12 422 5518

🕐 Mon–Sat 11.30–6 (the High Altar opens at 11.50), Sun 2–6; no visitors during Mass

🍽 None

♿ Few ramps

💷 Inexpensive

❓ Ticket office is opposite the side door on the other side of plac Mariacki

Pałac Krzysztofory

TOP 25

The Fontana Room (left); sculpture in the cellar (middle); a carriage in front of the palace (right)

THE BASICS

www.mhk.pl

H3

Rynek Główny 35

12 619 2300

Apr–Oct Mon 10–2, Tue–Sun 9–5; Nov–Mar Mon 10–2, Tue, Thu, Sat–Sun 9–4, Fri 10–5

Courtyard café, cellar club (€)

None

Inexpensive; free Mon

HIGHLIGHTS

● Fontana stucco ceilings
● Arcaded courtyard
● Exhibition on the history of Krakow
● Exhibition of Christmas cribs (*szopki*) in December from the first Thursday in the month

Is it a palace, a museum or a club? Built in the grand manner, the Krzysztofory Palace, home to a museum of Krakow's history and culture, has something for everyone, especially at Christmas.

Italian style Built in the 17th century on medieval foundations and named for Św. Krzysztof (St. Christopher), this grand house is arranged around an arcaded Tuscan courtyard; the second floor museum has fine stucco ceilings by Italian artist Baldassare Fontana. The great and the good have always stayed here, among them Stanisław August Poniatowski, the last king and duke of the Polish-Lithuanian Commonwealth. Later on, the palace was a hot-bed of revolutionary fervor, housing members of the National Government during the 1846 Krakow Uprising.

History and happenings Nowadays the palace is the headquarters of the Historical Museum of the City of Krakow and the permanent exhibition is about the history and culture of the city. There are also changing temporary exhibitions. The cellars host the latest cutting-edge music and theater, while the Fontana Room holds regular classical concerts.

Christmas story In December, children and adults compete in making Christmas cribs, which go on show at the palace. Most of these *szopki* are in the traditional shapes of Krakow's best-loved buildings, but originality abounds.

Bar in the cellar (left); dining room (right)

Restauracja Wierzynek

When you begin with a banquet attended by almost half the crowned heads of Europe, as Mikołaj Wierzynek did in 1364, it's a hard act to follow, yet heads of state and celebrities are welcomed at this restaurant to the present day.

Wedding feast Wierzynek's grand gesture—which he could well afford as a banker and mayor to the salt-rich district of Wieliczka—was to celebrate the marriage of the granddaughter of King Kazimierz the Great to Holy Roman Emperor Charles IV. The guests included the kings of Denmark, Hungary and Cyprus. Some say King Kazimierz had a diplomatic motive and wanted to ease growing political tensions in Europe. Whatever the reasons, a good time was had by all, and Wierzynek's gifts of silver plates to each guest also went down well with the nobility. So the king granted Wierzynek a permit to entertain future prominent visitors to the city, starting a tradition that continues today. Diners have included former American president George Bush Sr., former king of Spain Juan Carlos, and movie director Steven Spielberg.

Renaissance spirit The whole building has been expertly restored to Renaissance style, with splendid tiled stoves and coffered ceilings. Each of the restaurant's many rooms has a different theme, while the café has a lighter, more modern menu and decor; you can see Wierzynek's own well in the vaulted cellar bar. The main restaurant serves Old Polish cuisine.

THE BASICS

www.wierzynek.com.pl

⊞ H4

✉ Rynek Główny 15

☎ 12 424 9600

🕙 Daily 1–11

🍴 Restaurant (€€€), café (€€) and cellar bar and grill (€)

♿ Elevator

HIGHLIGHTS

● The Knights' Hall
● The visitors' book
● The view over the market square
● Princely service
● Wild boar, roe deer and roast sturgeon with Polish crayfish on the menu

TIP

● Though the café and cellar bar are more relaxed, reservations are recommended for the main restaurant.

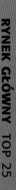

RYNEK GŁÓWNY TOP 25

29

Sukiennice

HIGHLIGHTS

● Renaissance and
Modernist gargoyles
● One-stop souvenir
shopping
● High-quality goods

DID YOU KNOW?

● The knife that the jealous builder of St. Mary's Watchtower used to kill his brother, builder of the bell tower, hangs on one of the walls.

TIP

● Don't haggle—it's not done in the Sukiennice. In any case, you'll find prices are no higher than in the rest of Krakow and many of the stalls, particularly those selling jewelry, are branches of shops elsewhere in the city.

In Krakow, even the main shopping mall, the Cloth Hall, dates from the 13th century. Today's stallholders have everything a souvenir hunter needs, from leather bags to wooden dragons.

Enterprise More than 100m (110 yards) long and sitting proudly in the main square, Krakow's ancient Cloth Hall emphasizes the central role of trade in the development of the city. The original medieval building was developed under Kazimierz the Great in the 14th century but, after a fire in the mid-16th century, was rebuilt in curvaceous Renaissance style with stone masks along the parapets. As time went on many other stalls and shacks were erected around it, until a grand sweep of town planning

Clockwise from far left: A café in the arcades; a stall selling icons; the exterior of the Cloth Hall; shoppers in the entrance arcade; stained-glass decorations

cleared them all away in the 19th century. The flower sellers in the square are the only outside traders who survived the clean-up.

Stalls The souvenirs on sale are good quality, mainly traditional Polish crafts: leather bags, sheepskins, small stained-glass angels, carved wooden figures, wooden boxes, jewelry, linen and embroidered folk costumes. Children may like the toy dragons and pint-sized chainmail.

Gallery The upper floor of the Cloth Hall is devoted to a gallery of 19th-century Polish art including about 450 paintings and many sculptures. The four renovated and rather under-visited halls contain some of the finest works of Polish art in the city.

THE BASICS

✚ H4

✉ Rynek Główny 1–3

☎ None

🕐 Souvenir stalls daily 10–8

🍴 Cafés in the arcades

♿ Few but flat access

👋 Free

Sukiennice Gallery

www.mnk.pl

✉ Sukiennice, Rynek Główny 3

☎ 12 433 5400

🕐 Tue–Sun 10–6

👋 Inexpensive

More to See

DOROŻKI

www.dorozki.krakow.pl

Drawn up along the edge of the main square, Krakow's horse-drawn cabs add a tang to the atmosphere that even the nearby flower stalls can't mask. The horses are beautifully turned out with tassels and plumes. Look at their hooves: Their shoes have a special rubber sole to protect their feet on the cobbled streets. Choose whichever one you like, no need to take the first in line.

🚩 H3 ✉ Rynek Główny ☎ 12 431 2520 (Mon–Fri 10–5) 🕐 Daily from early morning until the small hours 🍴 Cafés nearby 🚻 Big step up into the carriages 🎫 Expensive, the fixed price depends on the length of the journey: The shortest is around the main square, about 100PLN (€23); the longest a round-trip to Wawel and Kazimierz, about 300PLN (€70)

KAMIENICA HIPOLITÓW

www.mhk.pl

It's all very well looking at the facades of the nobility's houses, but how did they live? This museum demonstrates how wealthy families lived between the 17th and 19th centuries, though the house itself dates back to the 14th century.

🚩 J3 ✉ plac Mariacki 3 ☎ 12 422 4219 🕐 May–Oct Wed–Sun 10–5.30; Nov–Apr Wed, Fri–Sun 9–4, Thu 12–7. Closed 2nd Sun of month all year 🍴 Magia café at entrance 🚻 None 🎫 Inexpensive, free Wed

KOŚCIÓŁ ŚW. BARBARY

It's easy to overlook the modest entrance to St. Barbara's Church between the visitors' entrance to St. Mary's and the ticket office. Dating from the end of the 14th century, it is said that the church was built with the bricks left over from St. Mary's. Renovations are ongoing; the painted ceiling has already been restored to former glory. Look, too, for the early 15th-century Pietà and a crucifix from the same century on the high altar.

🚩 J4 ✉ Maly Rynek 8 ☎ None 🕐 Daily according to the times of services; German Mass Sun 7pm 🍴 Many cafés nearby 🚻 None 🎫 Free

Kościół św. Wojciecha

Piwnica Pod Baranami

KOŚCIÓŁ ŚW. WOJCIECHA

This little gem of a baroque church built on Romanesque foundations is one of the oldest buildings in Krakow and still much used by locals. The best way to visit is to sit quietly in a rear pew—you'll see everything at a glance, including the image of the saint whose name is usually given as St. Adalbert in English. A small archaeology museum under the church has finds from the church and square.

🚼 H4 ✉ Rynek Główny 3 ☎ 12 422 7100 ⏰ Museum Jun–Sep daily 10–4, but often closed if wet 🍴 Cafés in the square 🚫 None 💷 Inexpensive

PIWNICA POD BARANAMI

www.piwnicapodbaranami.pl
On the corner of ul. św. Anny and the main square, the grand house Dom Pod Baranami has harbored Poland's most famous cabaret since 1956. The vaulted brick cellar (piwnica) still hosts cabaret, but mostly it is an alehouse where you can drink in the atmosphere along with the beer. The rest of the "House under the Sign of the Rams" houses arts venues, including one of Krakow's best cinemas.

🚼 H4 ✉ Dom Pod Baranami, Rynek Główny 27 ☎ 12 421 2500 ⏰ Cabaret night Sat 9pm–last customer; bar daily 11am–last customer 🍴 Café/bar 🚫 None 💷 Inexpensive ❓ Book cabaret tickets in advance Mon–Fri 11–3 at 26 ul. św. Tomasza or ☎ 12 421 2500

POMNIK ADAMA MICKIEWICZA

Not only was Adam Mickiewicz Poland's greatest Romantic poet, he was also an activist who gave voice to the vision of the restoration of the Polish nation, dying in exile in 1855 while forming a Polish legion to fight for his homeland. His statue is a favorite meeting place for Cracovians. If you find his name a mouthful, try using his nickname, Adaś, as the locals do.

🚼 H4 ✉ Rynek Główny between Sukiennice and Szara Restaurant 🍴 Many cafés in the square 🚫 Flat access over cobbles 💷 Free

Horse-drawn carriage

Adam Mickiewicz statue

POMNIK PIOTRA SKRZYNECKI

The statue of Piotr Skrzynecki, sitting in a convivial pose outside the Vis-à-Vis bar, stops many a visitor who may go on to "share" a drink with the jolly bronze without knowing who he is. Of course, Krakow is the kind of place where one makes new friends very easily in bars, and the anarchic Skrzynecki was an exceptional example of this. In 1956, he founded a landmark institution in Krakow's rich theatrical heritage—the cabaret at the Piwnica Pod Baranami, which continues next door to this day. Skrzynecki died in 1997 but the flower he usually carries shows how fresh and important his memory is.

🔒 H4 ✉ Rynek Główny 29 🍴 Outside Vis-à-Vis bar ♿ Flat though cobbled access 💵 Free

WIEŻA RATUSZOWA

www.mhk.pl

The lions guarding the steps to Krakow's Town Hall tower must always have been as sleepy as they are today because the rest of the Town Hall, which had suffered many fires, ruins and rebuildings since 1316, was snatched away under their noses in 1820 during a general tidying-up of the main square. The tower itself, leaning badly by 1703, has been repaired so you can try climbing to the top. Although the steep stone stairs are narrow and ascend to about the same height at St. Mary's, there are spacious former council chambers on the way up in which to rest. At the top there are good views on three sides—towards Wawel Hill, Kopiec Kościuszko and past St. Mary's Church to Nowa Huta—with inexpensive telescopes provided. Inside you'll see the workings of the former and current (atomic) Town Hall clock.

🔒 H4 ✉ Rynek Główny 1 ☎ 12 426 4334 🕐 Daily May–Oct 10.30–6. Closed in winter 🍴 Café and theater in cellar ♿ None 💵 Inexpensive, buy tickets from Tourist Information Office on ground floor. Inexpensive photo permits extra

Wieża Ratuszowa

Piotr Skrzynecki statue

Around the Rynek Główny

This is where to take the pulse of the city. Listen out for the *hejnał* from St. Mary's Tower and look up to see the ornamental parapets.

DISTANCE: 800m (0.5 miles) **ALLOW:** 45 mins to 2 hours

START

WIEŻA RATUSZOWA
✚ H4

1 With your back to the giant bronze face by Igor Mitoraj, walk behind the Town Hall tower and left towards ul. Grodzka. On this side of the square are some of the grandest houses.

2 At the corner of ul. Grodzka look right down the Royal Route towards Wawel Hill. To your left is the tiny church of St. Adalbert (▷ 33).

3 Cross ul. Grodzka and walk left up the square. Pass the intellectuals' hang-out Pod Jaszczurami with its emblem of fighting lizards and glance into the "Alkohole" shop at No. 7—its vaulted ceiling is almost as lovely as that in the Kamienica Szara restaurant next door.

4 Before you reach St. Mary's Church (▷ 26–27) look right into the little square where you'll see a fountain with a statue of a medieval student, a copy of one of the figures from Veit Stoss's High Altar.

END

DOM POD BARANAMI
✚ H4

8 Make your way toward the "House under the Sign of the Rams" or Dom Pod Baranami (▷ 33) on the corner of ul. św. Anny.

7 Turning left at the Krzysztofory Palace (▷ 28) you'll find, set into the square opposite the end of ul. Szewska, a plaque showing where Kościuszko swore to serve his nation at the start of the 1794 Kościuszko Uprising against Russia.

6 At ul. Floriańska turn left.

5 To your left is the statue of Adam Mickiewicz (▷ 33). You are now walking towards ul. Floriańska, the other half of the Royal Route, which offers a splendid vista ending in St. Florian's Gate and the Barbican.

Shopping

ALHENA
Just outside the main market square, this sparkling shop has an excellent selection of modern Polish glass as well as the more tradition crystal, all handmade in the Małopolska town of Krosno, sometimes known as "little Krakow."
 J4 ✉ plac Mariacki 1 ☎ 12 421 5496 🕐 Mon–Fri 10–7, Sat 11–3

DELICATESY
www.podwawelska.pl
Next to the Wawel chocolate shop, this handy food shop (whose official name is Podwawelska Spółdzielnia Spożywców) has a wide range of sweets, biscuits, Polish sausages and cheeses—a good place to find Polish delicacies to take home as well as everyday food.
➕ H3 ✉ Rynek Główny 34 ☎ 12 428 0575 🕐 Daily 7am–10pm, Sun 10–10

KSIĘGARNIA CAMENA
Although it's a bookstore with little available in English, this is worth visiting for the CD selection, which is particularly strong on classical music, both traditional and contemporary composers.
➕ H3 ✉ Rynek Główny 34 ☎ 12 422 6023 🕐 Daily 10–7

PASAŻ 13
www.pasaz-13.pl
Aimed at business travelers, this petite, upscale shopping mall directly on Rynek Główny contains some of the top names of the retail world, as well as an aromatic deli selling food from across the globe, a couple of snazzy bars, a wine cellar and a pricey café. Staff generally speak English.
➕ H4 ✉ Rynek Główny 12–13 ☎ 12 617 0250 🕐 Mon–Sat 9–9, Sun 11–5

SUKIENNICE
If your time is limited, shop here for souvenirs and jewelry. Prices are no higher, the quality is good and the whole range of local arts and crafts is on sale. Many of the stalls, especially those selling jewelry, are branches of shops elsewhere in the city.

FOREVER AMBER
Amber, or *bursztyn,* has been bought and sold here since Roman times, when the main trade routes ran from the Baltic to the Mediterranean and to Asia along the Silk Road. Baltic amber, the solidified resin of prehistoric pine trees, was found in Tutankhamun's tomb and was also used as an offering at the temple at Delphi. Don't buy for investment unless you are an expert, and remember it's not as tough as gemstones. An insect trapped in amber makes an unusual piece.

➕ H3–4 ✉ Rynek Główny 1–3 🕐 Daily 10–8

SZAMBELAN
www.szambelan.pl
A short distance from Rynek Główny, this tiny laboratory-like shop sells the famous Polish vodka flavored with various herbs, fruit, flowers and other ingredients, as well as a range of oils, jams and vinegars.
➕ H4 ✉ ul. Bracka 9 ☎ 12 628 7093 🕐 Mon–Thu 11–8, Fri–Sat 11–8.30, Sun 12–6

WAWEL
www.wawel-sklep.com.pl
This sweet shop is a Polish institution, with branches throughout the country. Look out for chocolate-covered plums, praline-centered Michałki and chestnut-flavored Kasztanki. Chocolates, sweets and biscuits are sold by weight and also in elegant presentation boxes, of which the most typical is the Królewski Smak (Royal Taste) selection.
➕ H3 ✉ Rynek Główny 33 ☎ 12 423 1247 🕐 Daily 10–7

ZEBRA
If sightseeing has been too hard on your feet, come here for a large selection of well-priced men's and women's shoes, both fashionable and practical.
➕ H4 ✉ Rynek Główny 7 ☎ 12 421 4034 🕐 Mon–Sat 10–8, Sun 10.30–6

Entertainment and Nightlife

BONEROWSKI PALACE

www.pro-arts.pl
Weekly 90-minute Chopin recitals are performed in this noble mansion, now restored to former glory.
🔼 H3 ✉ ul. św. Jana 1
☎ 12 374 1300 🕐 Sat 7pm

BORO

Relax on the leather sofas of this three-room courtyard-level club in the Pod Baranami building for coffee early on, and DJs and live music later.
🔼 H4 ✉ Rynek Główny 27
☎ 693 922 010 🕐 Nightly 5pm–last customer

DOM POLONIA

www.orfeusz.eu
This smart central location stages Chopin piano recitals lasting about 80 minutes by well-known performers. Other shows, including Polish folk performances and Jewish music concerts, are sometimes held, mainly in summer.
🔼 H4 ✉ Rynek Główny 14
☎ 662 007 255 🕐 Chopin concerts daily 6pm

HARRIS PIANO JAZZ BAR

www.harris.krakow.pl
This cellar bar often has more atmosphere than air. Polish and international live bands perform several times a week.
🔼 H4 ✉ Rynek Główny 28 ☎ 12 421 5741, reservations possible 🕐 Mon–Fri 1pm–last customer, Sat–Sun 11am–last customer

KINO POD BARANAMI

www.kinopodbaranami.pl
This two-screen art-house cinema in the Potocki Palace is dedicated to quality films from around the world.
🔼 H4 ✉ Rynek Główny 27
☎ 12 423 0768 🕐 Daily 12–12

KRZYSZTOFORY PALACE

www.classica.krakow.pl
Come here for classical music (featuring more than just Chopin) played by the Cracow Philharmonic Quartet in the 17th-century Fontana Room upstairs, hung with portraits of the Polish nobility. Meanwhile, the cellar hosts regular club nights with adventurous music tending towards electronica. In summer, clubbers can spill out into the courtyard to chill.

🔼 H3 ✉ Rynek Główny 35; cellar club enter from ul. Szczepańska 2 ☎ Classical concerts: 501 638 750; cellar club: 12 422 2236 🕐 Classical concerts Sun 7pm; other classical music concerts usually Wed and Sat; nightly cellar club nights 5pm–last customer

THE PIANO ROUGE

www.thepianorouge.com
The red carpet down to this elegant three-room air-conditioned cellar club, bar and restaurant sets the tone for live music—pop, blues and standards as well as jazz.
🔼 H3 ✉ Rynek Główny 46
☎ 12 431 0333 🕐 Sun–Thu 9pm–2am, Fri–Sat 9pm–4am

POD JASZCZURAMI

www.podjaszczurami.pl
This studenty bar "Under the Sign of the Lizards" has been buzzing since 1969. It has an ever-changing schedule that includes music, debates, lectures and movies and other events.
🔼 H4 ✉ Rynek Główny 8
☎ 12 429 4538 🕐 Mon–Wed 10am–1am, disco nights Thu–Sat 10am–4am, Sun 11am–1am

SHOWTIME

Live bands play nightly among the crimson seats and zebra heads. A varied music policy tends toward pop and rock for over-21s.
🔼 H3 ✉ Rynek Główny 28
☎ 12 421 4714 🕐 Sun–Thu 7pm–2am; Fri–Sat 7pm–4am

Restaurants

DA PIETRO (€€)

www.dapietro.pl
Krakow's first Italian job is still going strong after two decades of serving top-notch pastas, pizzas and seafood to tourists and locals alike.
✚ H4 ✉ Rynek Główny 17 ☎ 12 422 3279 🕐 Daily 10.30am–midnight

EUROPEJSKA (€€)

www.europejska.pl
This smart café has a long menu and a decor that harks back to a more formal age. Its Euro theme is completed by an English phone box and French horn.
✚ H3 ✉ Rynek Główny 35 ☎ 12 429 3493 🕐 Daily 8am–midnight

HAWEŁKA (€€€)

www.hawelka.pl
Once a kind of Cracovian Harrods, Pod Palmą (Under the Palm Tree) is now a traditional restaurant serving Polish classics in a smart room with an even more upscale salon, Restaurant Tetmajerowska, above.
✚ H3 ✉ Rynek Główny 34 ☎ 12 422 0631 🕐 Daily 11–11

KAWIARNIA RATUSZOWA (€)

The café in the basement of the Town Hall tower spreads out into the main square in summer—making it a great choice for people-watching.
✚ H4 ✉ Rynek Główny 1 ☎ 12 421 1326 🕐 Daily 9am–midnight

RESTAURACJA SZARA (€€)

www.szara.pl
This is one of the most beautiful rooms on the square, with a Belle Époque ambience under a lofty vaulted ceiling. The international menu with a Polish accent features delicacies like smoked reindeer tartare and butter-fried pike-perch.

GAME ON

In contrast to the more inexpensive eating places elsewhere in the Old Town which are heavy on dumplings and other carbs, the premier restaurants in the Rynek Główny highlight traditional ingredients gathered from the wild. This is the place to try boar, boletus mushrooms or pike-perch. You might find a menu featuring grilled saddle of fallow deer with bacon or a starter of *rydze* (milk-cap mushrooms). Sophisticated rather than rustic, the flavors are often reminiscent of the best Italian cooking.

✚ H4 ✉ Rynek Główny 6 ☎ 12 421 6669 🕐 Daily 11–11

WENTZL (€€€)

www.restauracjawentzl.com
This many-roomed restaurant has been here since 1792 and its Renaissance salons are crammed with pictures of celebrated diners. Chef Grzegorz Zdeb's Polish and French specialties include wild boar fillet marinated in wild berry sauce with honey liqueur and roasted garlic.
✚ H4 ✉ Rynek Główny 19 ☎ 12 429 5299 🕐 Daily 12–11

WESELE (€€)

www.weselerestauracja.pl
Authentic Polish cooking done just the way it should be is the star turn at this two-level Rynek restaurant decorated in romantically Polish fashion.
✚ H4 ✉ Rynek Główny 10 ☎ 12 307 8700 🕐 Daily 12–11

WIERZYNEK (€€€)

www.wierzynek.com.pl
The oldest restaurant in Krakow (▷ 29) is now evolving to cater to modern tastes with accomplished and contemporary food that respects its tradition. Expert service delivers consistent quality in seven rooms.
✚ H4 ✉ Rynek Główny 15 ☎ 12 424 9600 🕐 Daily 1–11

Krakow's Old Town holds more than enough treasures to keep you busy for a week. Here you'll find university buildings, a fine art collection and dozens of medieval and baroque churches.

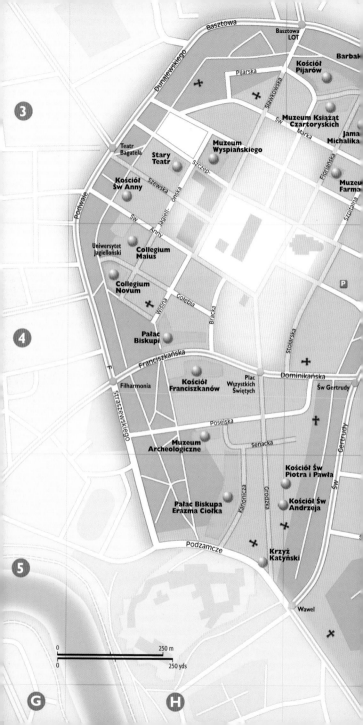

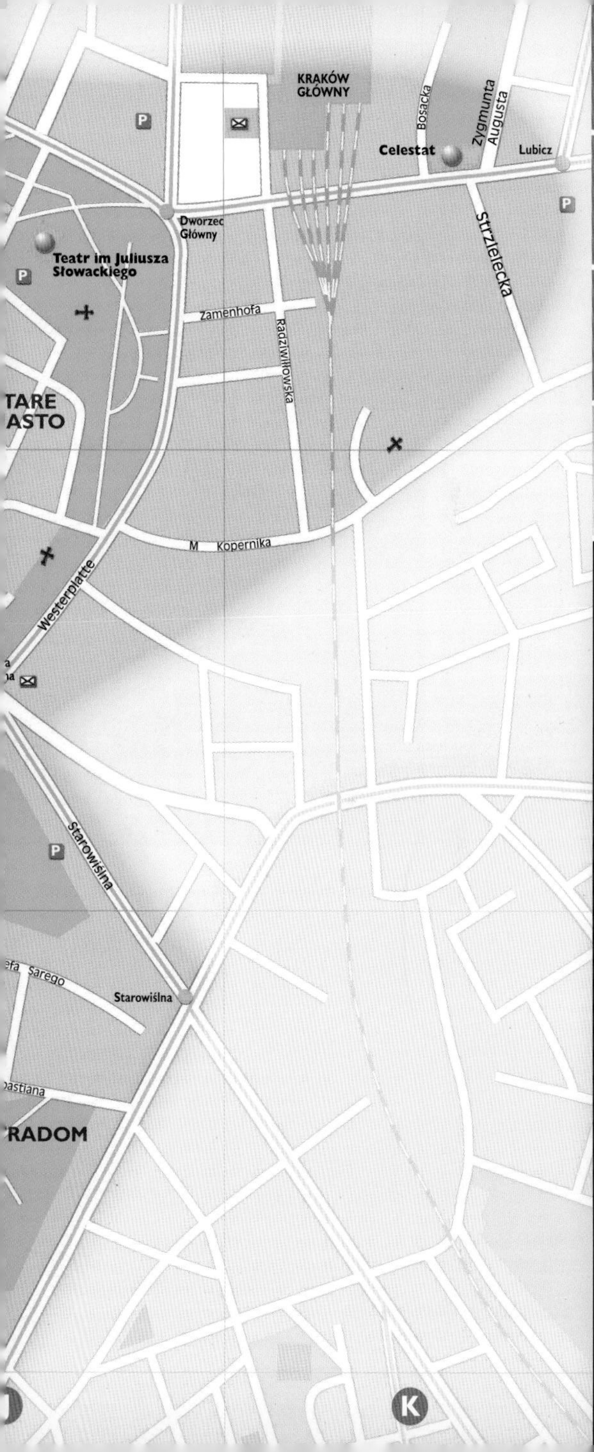

KRAKÓW
GŁÓWNY

Bosacka

Zygmunta
Augusta

Celestat

Lubicz

P

Strzelecka

Dworzec
Główny

Teatr im Juliusza
Słowackiego

P

Zamenhofa

Radziwiłłowska

TARE
ASTO

M Kopernika

Westerplatte

Starowiślna

P

Starowiślna

fa sarego

Starowiślna

astiana

RADOM

J

K

Collegium Maius

HIGHLIGHTS

● Musical clock
● Jagiellonian Globe of 1508, the first to show America
● Wooden carving of Kazimierz the Great from about 1380
● Astrolabe from Cordoba made in 1054
● 17th-century Persian carpets
● Rector's gold chain dating from AD500
● Polish director Andrzej Wajda's Oscar
● Mementoes of Moon landings

DID YOU KNOW?

● The figures on the court-yard clock were carved in the 1950s and the clock is computer controlled. It plays at 9am, 11am, 1pm, 3pm and 5pm.
● Visit the cellar coffee shop U Pęcherza (☎ 12 663 1518 ⊙ Mon–Fri 7–5, Sat 8–5, Sun 9–5) and you'll be in the oldest part of the building.

The oldest university building in Poland, the Collegium Maius sums up the history of learning in this city of more than 40,000 students—and has some modern surprises in its museum.

Ancient lessons The Krakow Academy, which pre-dated the university, was founded in 1364 by Kazimierz the Great. It was revived here by Queen Jadwiga, who gave her crown jewels to fund it, and her husband King Władysław Jagiellon, who donated this building in 1400. There was a clock in the courtyard even then, but the musical clock that plays the university song, *Gaudeamus Igitur*, daily while university figures walk round the dial, is 20th century.

Old studies Upstairs in the Library beneath its traditionally painted ceiling, you'll see portraits

Clockwise from far left: Painted ceiling in the Library; the courtyard; detail of a water feature; the figures of the musical clock

of the university's eminent scholars. Then come professors' rooms, complete with period furniture and an enormous variety of objects and treasures from the university's beginnings up to the present day. The Stuba Communis, or refectory, features a 14th-century sculpture of Kazimierz the Great; the Treasury has three 15th-century scepters and the only preserved drawing by Veit Stoss, creator of the altar in St. Mary's Church. A whole room is dedicated to the revolutionary astronomer Nicholas Copernicus, who studied here from 1491 to 1495. The Jagiellonian Hall, which now has a purely ceremonial function, movingly displays portraits of some of the professors who were murdered by the Nazis. After all the "look, don't touch" displays, children particularly may enjoy getting their hands on the separate interactive World of the Senses science exhibition.

THE BASICS

www.uj.edu.pl/muzeum
www.maius.uj.edu.pl
➕ H4
✉ ul. Jagiellońska 15
☎ 12 422 0549, 12 663 1307
🕐 Main exhibition 30-min tours Mon, Wed–Fri 10–2.20, Tue 10–3.20. Main exhibition plus scientific and fine arts collections, hour-long tour Mon–Fri only 1pm. World of the Senses Mon–Sat 9–1.30
🍴 Cellar café (€)
♿ Good
🎟 Main exhibition inexpensive, free Apr–Sep Tue 3–5.20; longer tour with scientific and fine arts collections moderate; World of the Senses inexpensive, Sat free
❓ Advance booking recommended, especially for tours in English: main Collegium Maius tours tel 12 663 1521; World of the Senses tel 12 663 1319

Jama Michalika

Glass ceiling by Karol Frycz (left); the sumptuous interior (right)

THE BASICS

www.jamamichalika.pl

🚩 J3

✉ ul. Floriańska 45

☎ 12 422 1561

🕐 Sun–Thu 9am–10pm, Fri, Sat 9am–11pm

💷 Inexpensive

♿ Main room is on ground floor

HIGHLIGHTS

● Green balloon still hanging from the ceiling
● Century-old marionettes from the popular satirical Christmas shows
● Art nouveau stained glass
● Cakes, especially *sernik* (cheesecake) and Wawel cake

While not the oldest such establishment in the city, this is the one that sums up what Krakow café society is all about. People, the arts and fashion have moved on, but this place showed them the way.

Cabaret set "Michal's Den" was set up in 1895, and soon attracted the cream of the city's writers, artists and actors. Within a decade it had become the home of Zielony Balonik—the Green Balloon cabaret—which poked fun at the bourgeoisie of the day. At the same time, it became the unofficial headquarters and meeting place of the Młoda Polska, or Young Poland, movement. The art nouveau furniture and furnishings of the café are still much as they were in its heyday. The walls hung with paintings, puppets, caricatures and all manner of artwork reinforce the fin-de-siècle atmosphere. Of course, a green balloon takes pride of place.

Café chat Though today it's more frequented by the middle-aged middle class gossiping over cheesecake than wild bohemians, Jama Michalika is a good starting point from which to explore Krakow's café society. There are hundreds of cafés in the Old Town alone and they have nothing in common with the global chains that have taken over other European cities, or with each other. Most are small, many open late—often until the last guest leaves—and nearly all serve alcohol as well as coffee, snacks and homemade cake. Now, as ever, the patrons provide the entertainment.

Kościół Franciszkanów

Painted ceiling by Wyspiański (left); the exterior of the church (middle); Wyspiański's stained glass (right)

After being almost destroyed in the great fire of 1850, the 13th-century Franciscan Church was redecorated early in the 20th century by the celebrated artists Stanisław Wyspiański and Józef Mehoffer.

New for old More than any other, the Franciscan Church demonstrates how Krakow's artists, while remaining resolutely contemporary, engage with the history of the city to restore and enliven it. Built between 1237 and 1269 by Henry the Pious for the newly arrived Franciscan monks, this was one of the first brick churches in the city. Damaged by Swedish invasions, the church was rebuilt again in baroque style, only to be destroyed in the great fire of Krakow, and then rebuilt in a mixture of styles. Duke Władysław Jagiellon, husband of Queen Jadwiga, was baptized here in 1386.

Art of glass Sit in the main body of the church for a while to appreciate the beautiful stylized flowers and stars painted on the walls and ceilings, the work of Wyspiański, who also created the stained-glass windows. But older treasures have survived. Look in the side chapels for the tomb of Giovanni Gemma, court Venetian physician who died in 1608, and the earlier Virgin Mary surrounded by angels. Outside, you'll find a modern artwork—seven stone and steel angels by Michał Batkiewicz, which appear to be praying toward the window across the street from which Pope John Paul II used to greet the faithful when he was Archbishop of Krakow.

THE BASICS

➕ H4

✉ plac Wszystkich Świętych 5

☎ 12 422 5376

🕐 Daily 6am–7.45pm

♿ None

💷 Free

HIGHLIGHTS

● Gothic, Renaissance and baroque murals in the cloisters
● Mehoffer's 1933 Stations of the Cross
● Wyspiański's art nouveau window *God the Father—Become!*
● Wyspiański's flower-painted walls and ceilings
● Master Jerzy's 16th-century *Mater Dolorosa*

TIP

● You can see changes in the stained-glass windows as the light strikes them at different times of day.

Muzeum Książąt Czartoryskich

HIGHLIGHTS

● Da Vinci's *Lady with an Ermine*
● Rembrandt's *Landscape with the Good Samaritan*
● Armor, weaponry and tents captured by Polish troops from the Turks at the Battle of Vienna in 1683
● Roslin's 1774 portrait of Princess Izabela in Paris
● Portraits of Jagielloń Family, *c*.1556, School of Cranach the Younger
● Gallery of Early Antiquities, with early Christian, Roman, Etruscan, Greek and Egyptian objects

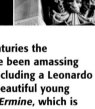

DID YOU KNOW?

● There is debate over the animal depicted in Leonardo da Vinci's portrait *Lady with an Ermine*. When she first saw it Princess Izabela said, "If it is a dog, it is a very ugly one."

For more than two centuries the Czartoryski family have been amassing choice pieces of art, including a Leonardo da Vinci portrait of a beautiful young woman, *Lady with an Ermine*, which is easily the match of the more famous *Mona Lisa* in Paris.

Patriotic princess With the idea of preserving Poland's heritage, Princess Izabela Czartoryska began collecting art and curiosities at her palace at Pulawy in the late 18th century. Among the first items the heiress bought were Turkish trophies from the siege of Vienna a century before, and Polish royal treasures from Wawel, looted in earlier times. But she was a romantic magpie and soon added Shakespeare's chair, bits of the grave of Romeo and Juliet, the ashes

Clockwise from far left: Rembrandt's Landscape with the Good Samaritan; *an archway joins the museum's buildings; the museum's exterior; Roman busts on display; the Czartoryski coat of arms;* Lady with an Ermine *by Leonardo da Vinci*

of El Cid and his wife, and relics of Abelard and Héloïse, and Petrarch and Laura. By 1798, her son Prince Adam Jerzy, traveling in Italy, had acquired da Vinci's *Lady with an Ermine* and Raphael's *Portrait of a Young Man*, which became the jewels of the collection. Living in exile in Paris, her descendants added to the collection. In 1876, the city of Krakow offered its old arsenal as a home for the collection, and the museum was born.

War torn In World War II, the best pieces were taken by the Nazis for Hitler's private collection, while the curator died in a concentration camp. Many of the items were later returned, though 844 of them are still missing, including the precious Raphael. An empty frame hangs in the museum awaiting its return.

THE BASICS

www.muzeum-czartoryskich.krakow.pl

www.czartoryski.org

➕ J3

✉ ul. św. Jana 19; entrance also at ul. Pijarska 8

☎ 12 422 5566

🕐 Tue–Sat 10–6, Sun 10–4. Closed Dec and some hols

♿ None

🎟 Inexpensive, Sun free

TIP

● Remember that, as in all Krakow's museums, the last ticket is sold half an hour before closing. This rule is very strictly enforced here.

Muzeum Wyspiańskiego

Model of Wawel Hill as an Acropolis (left); Self Portrait with Wife, 1904 (middle); detail of a staircase (right)

THE BASICS

www.mnk.pl

⊞ H3

✉ plac Szczepański 9

☎ 12 292 8183,
12 422 7021

🕐 Tue–Sat 10–6, Sun 10–4

🍴 Café (€)

♿ Few to temporary exhibitions on ground floor

👋 Inexpensive; free Sun

HIGHLIGHTS

● Wyspiański's model of Wawel Hill as a Polish Acropolis
● *Planty with a View onto Wawel*, oil, 1894
● Bannisters and cartoon of a window showing *Apollo for the Medical House*
● Pastel portrait of Wyspiański's daughter, *Little Helena*
● Interior design for the apartment of Tadeusz "Boy" Żeleński, a doctor, translator and writer
● Last self-portrait, 1907

Born in the city in 1869, the son of a sculptor, Stanisław Wyspiański left his mark everywhere in Krakow, as a painter, playwright, sculptor, designer and professor. The Szołayski House is where all these strands are drawn together.

Star pupil Wyspiański began his short but creative life—he died of syphilis aged 38—by studying art history at the Jagiellonian University and painting at the Academy of Fine Arts. There he was taught by Jan Matejko, who soon engaged his student to help him renovate St. Mary's Church in the Rynek Główny. By 1890, the young artist had embarked on a tour of Europe, studying in Paris for three years, where he mingled with artists he admired such as Gauguin and Puvis de Chavannes and shared a studio with his compatriot Józef Mehoffer.

Home boy Returning to Krakow, Wyspiański plunged into city life, taking his home town and the Polish nation as his main themes. He seemed to work on everything: stained-glass windows for the Dominican and Franciscan churches; a costume for the Lajkonik folk figure that is still used today; a complete redesign for the buildings on Wawel Hill; portraits; art criticism; posters; and plays, including one called *Wesele (The Wedding)*, censored at the time, which is now much admired. Through it all he was a moving spirit in the Młoda Polksa, or Young Poland movement, which paralleled the wider European Modernist movement.

Lanterns in memory of Pope John Paul II (left); a portrait of John Paul II (middle); an entranceway (right)

Pałac Biskupa Erazma Ciołka

As well as housing superb collections of sacred art, this restored palace in Krakow's oldest and best-preserved street has many original medieval and Renaissance details.

Carved beauty One of most beautiful houses in Krakow, Bishop Erazm Ciołek's Palace dates from the beginning of the 16th century. Today his residence contains two exhibitions of religious art. The Art of Old Poland rooms are prefaced by a small group of 12th-century stone carvings discovered in local churches and cloisters. There follows a collection of wooden Madonnas, saints and altars dating from the 14th to 16th centuries, also from churches in the region. One room is devoted to the work of Veit Stoss, the master carver of St. Mary's altar.

Sacred icons The second exhibition, of Orthodox art of the old Polish-Lithuanian Republic, comprises a priceless collection of 15th- and 16th-century Carpathian icons, plus later icons showing the Renaissance and baroque influence that came once the Orthodox Church had accepted Rome in 1596.

Pope's progress The Archdiocesan Museum next door has a large collection of sacred art on display and a reconstruction of the rooms of the future Pope John Paul II, who lived in the beautiful Deanery at No. 21 as a priest in the 1950s. The new John Paul II Center (www.janpawel2.pl) stands opposite at No. 18.

THE BASICS

www.muzeum.krakow.pl

⊞ H5

✉ ul. Kanonicza 17

☎ 12 429 1558, 12 424 9370

🕐 Mon–Fri 10–4

♿ Very good, elevators and ramps to most sections

🎫 Art of Old Poland gallery inexpensive; Orthodox Art gallery inexpensive; combined ticket moderate

HIGHLIGHTS

● Madonna of Krużlowa, c. 1410
● *St. Hieronymus* by Hans Dürer (brother of Albrecht)
● Padovano angels of 1533
● 16th-century wooden statue of Christ riding a donkey
● Mandylion, imprint of Christ's face on a cloth
● Karol Wojtyła's rooms in Archdiocesan Museum
● Archdiocesan Museum's Małopolska Madonnas

More to See

BARBAKAN

www.mhk.pl

This grand fortification protected the old Royal Route that led to Wawel Hill and also formed part of an important trade route. First raised at the end of the 15th century, today it stands like an isolated fort. Climb into the upper galleries for a good view over the city. In summer (Jun–Sep) there are regular medieval pageants and knightly combats inside.

➕ J3 ✉ ul. Basztowa ☎ 12 422 9877
🕐 15 Apr–Oct daily 10.30–5 ♿ None
♿ Inexpensive (ticket also gives entry to the city walls and the Celestat Museum)

BRAMA FLORIAŃSKA

From 1300 Florian's Gate is where future kings of Poland traditionally entered the city on their way to be crowned at Wawel Cathedral. Today you can visit the remaining city walls either side of the gate and read interesting explanations of how each guild of city tradesmen had its own defensive part to play. The haberdashers and carpenters seem to have made a pretty good job of it, coached by the Marksmen's Guild.

➕ J3

CELESTAT

www.mhk.pl

This uniquely Cracovian institution will only make sense if you have already visited the city walls. This is the headquarters of the Marksmen's Guild, known as the Bratstwo Kurkowe or Brotherhood of the Cockerel, who for centuries have been the city's ace sharpshooters. Here you'll find a rifle range and a museum of the guild's history, with pride of place given to a Renaissance silver cockerel.

➕ K3 ✉ ul. Lubicz 16 ☎ 12 429 3791
🕐 May–Oct Tue, Thu–Sat and second Sun of month 9.30–5, Wed 9–4; Nov–Apr Tue–Wed, Fri–Sat, second Sun of month 9–4, Thu 11–6 ♿ Good, ground floor, wide doors ♿ Inexpensive; includes admission to Barbican and city walls

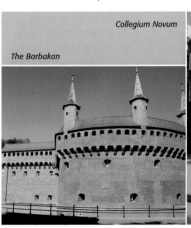

The Barbakan

Collegium Novum

COLLEGIUM NOVUM

This grand, red-brick university administrative building was constructed in the 1880s on the site of the 15th-century Jerusalem and Philosophers' halls of residence. All the university's big ceremonies take place in its Aula Magna, or Great Hall, which is hung with magnificent paintings. You may see graduates in traditional robes having their photos taken outside, but your best chance of seeing the Aula is to attend a concert there.

➕ H4 ✉ ul. Gołębia 24 🕐 Not open to tourists, view outside only from the Planty, unless attending a concert ♿ Planty access flat, ul. Gołębia cobbled

KOŚCIÓŁ ŚW. ANDRZEJA

Dating from the end of the 11th century, St. Andrew's is an unusual Romanesque survival in a city remade in Gothic and later styles—perhaps because it was the only church in the city to escape the mass destruction of the Tatar invasion of 1241. Even so, its

two white towers are topped with baroque cupolas, and inside you'll find baroque stucco by Baldassare Fontana, an ebony and silver tabernacle and a pulpit in the shape of a boat.

➕ J5 ✉ ul. Grodzka 56 🕐 Daily 7.30–5 🍴 Café nearby ♿ None 💲 Free

KOŚCIÓŁ ŚW. ANNY

A high point of baroque in Krakow, the university church of St. Anne's was built at the end of the 17th century. Once your eyes have taken in the dazzling gilded and painted cupola and the pulpit held aloft by gold angels, you may be able to discern the main altar, sculpted by Baldassare Fontana and dedicated to św. Jan Kęnty, a professor and saint buried here in 1473.

➕ H3 ✉ ul. św. Anny 11 ☎ 12 422 5318 🕐 Daily 7am–9pm 🍴 Cafés nearby ♿ None 💲 Free

KOŚCIÓŁ PIJARÓW

Rising ornately at the end of ul. św. Jana, the rococo facade of

Detail of the pulpit in St. Andrew's

Kościół św. Anny

the Piarist Church was added by Francesco Placidi about 30 years after the church was built at the beginning of the 18th century, while the restored interior features magnificent *trompe-l'oeil* paintings by Franz Eckstein. The atmospheric crypt is often used for concerts and exhibitions.

🕂 J3 ✉ ul. Pijarska 2 🕐 Daily 7–7 ♿ None

KOŚCIÓŁ ŚW. PIOTRA I PAWŁA

Consecrated in 1635 and the first completely baroque church in Poland, SS. Peter and Paul is easy to recognize from the line of statues of the apostles that separates it from ul. Grodzka. Inside, you'll find fine baroque detail in the stuccowork, tombs and organ loft. There's also a model of Foucault's Pendulum, which demonstrates the rotation of the Earth. Jesuit preacher Piotr Skarga, whose statue dominates Plac św. Marii Magdaleny opposite, is buried in the crypt.

🕂 J5 ✉ ul. Grodzka 54 🕐 Daily 7–7, later for concerts; demonstration of Foucault's Pendulum Thu 10, 11, 12 ♿ None

KRZYŻ KATYŃSKI

At the end of ul. Grodzka, outside the 14th-century Kościół św. Idziego (St. Giles), a simple wooden cross commemorates the massacre in the forest of Katyń in March 1940 of some 22,000 Polish officers by Russian troops. The victims included many academics, doctors and lawyers, in accordance with Stalin's aim to eliminate Poland's leaders and intelligentsia.

🕂 H5 ✉ ul. św. Idziego 1

MAŁY RYNEK

Its name translates as Small Market Square, and this quiet space behind St. Mary's Church has a forgotten air, despite its many cafés and bars. Yet there was a market here before Rynek Główny was laid out. Today it's of interest mainly for the fine noblemen's houses that line three of its sides.

🕂 J4 ✉ Mały Rynek 🍴 Cafés (€)

Muzeum Archeologiczne

Dome of SS. Peter and Paul

MUZEUM ARCHEOLOGICZNE
www.ma.krakow.pl

See Egyptian mummies and more from around the world. Highlights include finds from the local Małopolska region such as Światowid, an early pagan idol resembling a stone totem pole.

➕ H4 ✉ ul. Senacka 3; enter garden and museum from ul. Poselska 3 ☎ 12 422 7100, 12 422 7560 🕓 Jul–Aug Mon–Fri 11–6, Sun 10–3; Sep–Jun Mon, Wed, Fri 9–3, Tue, Thu 9–6, Sun 11–4 🍴 None ♿ Few 🥤 Inexpensive; permanent exhibition free Sun; English audio guide inexpensive; garden inexpensive

MUZEUM DOM POD KRZYŻEM
www.mhk.pl

Normally the "House under the Cross," a grand Renaissance building formerly variously used as a hospital or a monastery, hosts an exhibition about the history of theater in Krakow, but it is under renovation and no date has yet been set for its reopening.

➕ J3 ✉ ul. Szpitalna 21 ☎ 12 422 6864

MUZEUM FARMACJI
www.muzeumfarmacji.pl

The Pharmacy Museum is a fascinating collection of examples of the apothecary's art. The 22,000 exhibits, including pills, potions and instruments, are displayed over several floors from cellar to attic of a lovely building that still shows traces of a history going back to the 15th century. Under the Renaissance ceilings, pickled snakes and strange herbs share shelves with jars of leeches, while the basement is an alchemist's laboratory complete with dried bats and crocodiles. It's said that Faust studied at the Jagiellonian University, though whether Krakow is where he sold his soul to the devil is not known.

➕ J3 ✉ ul. Floriańska 25 ☎ 12 422 4284 🕓 Tue 12–6.30, Wed–Sun 12–2.30 🍴 None ♿ None 🥤 Inexpensive

PAŁAC BISKUPI

The bishops of Krakow have lived on this site since the 14th century, but today this 17th-century

Bottles inside the Muzeum Farmacji

Muzeum Dom Pod Krzyżem

building opposite the Franciscan Church attracts reverence as the residence of the Archbishop of Krakow, Karol Wojtyła, later Pope John Paul II, from 1963 to 1978. He conducted his celebrated conversations with the young people of Krakow and blessed the faithful from the "Pope's Window" over the main doorway.

➕ H4 ✉ ul. Franciszkańska 3

POMNIK KOPERNIKA

The statue of Copernicus near the Collegium Novum represents the great astronomer as a young man when he first studied astronomy at the Krakow Academy between 1491 and 1495, though he did not publish his revolutionary theory that the Earth orbits the sun until 1543.

➕ H4 ✉ ul. Gołębia/Planty ♿ Smooth paths in the Planty

STARY TEATR

www.stary.pl

Well restored to its 1905 art nouveau splendor after being left in a ruined state by World War II, the Old Theater was created in the late 18th century from several older buildings. A frieze by Józef Gardecki decorates the outside, while inside the ceilings are painted with flowers and the walls lined with portraits and busts of the greatest names in Polish theater.

➕ H3 ✉ ul. Jagiellońska 5 ☎ 12 422 4040 🕐 Museum Tue–Sat 11–1 and from an hour before curtain-up 🍴 Café Maska (€) (☎ 12 429 6044 🕐 Mon–Sat 9am–3am, Sun 11am–3am) ♿ Few 🎫 Tickets moderate

TEATR IM JULIUSZA SŁOWACKIEGO

www.slowacki.krakow.pl

Built in the 1890s, the Slowacki Theater, which can seat 900, is a great wedding-cake of a building, modeled on the Paris Opera by Jan Zawiejski and encrusted with detail.

➕ J3 ✉ plac św. Ducha 1 ☎ 12 424 4525 🕐 Box office Mon 10–2, 2.30–6, Tue–Sat 9–2, 2.30–7, Sun 3–7 🍴 Café (€) ♿ Few 🎫 Tickets moderate

The Slowacki Theater

Statue of Copernicus at the Collegium Novum

A Stroll around the Planty

In the 1800s, Krakow's crumbling city walls were replaced by a leafy green ring of gardens shaded by trees and ideal for strolling.

DISTANCE: 4km (2.5 miles) **ALLOW:** 1.5–2.5 hours

START

PLAC WSZYSTKICH ŚWIĘTYCH
H4 🚊 Tram to ul. Dominikańska

1 From the new Pawilon Wyspiański 2000, where you can see the artist's previously unrealized designs in stained glass, turn right, crossing ul. Grodzka into ul. Dominikańska, then turn left up the quiet backwater of ul. Stolarska.

2 Crossing Mały Rynek, walk along ul. Szpitalna and turn left after Teatr Słowackiego (▷ 54). Continue on ul. Pijarska along the remaining part of the city wall, with its open-air art gallery.

3 At St. Florian's Gate look left along ul. Floriańska to take in the vista enjoyed by successive kings of Poland on their way down the Royal Route to be crowned on Wawel Hill.

4 Continue along ul. Pijarska. At the Czartoryski Museum (▷ 46–47) with its second-floor bridge to the Arsenal, turn left down ul. św. Jana.

END

RYNEK GŁÓWNY
H4 🚊 Tram to ul. Dominikańska

8 Turn left up ul. Kanonicza, then cross plac św. Marii Magdaleny and go left up ul. Grodzka.

7 At ul. Gołębia turn right towards Collegium Novum (▷ 51) then left at the statue of Copernicus (▷ 54) and wander through the Planty down to ul. Podzamcze, where you turn left.

6 At ul. św. Anny, turn left, then right down ul. Jagiellońska past the Collegium Maius (▷ 42–43). Look into the courtyard to see the clock.

5 At plac św. Tomasza, where there is a little group of good restaurants, turn right along ul. św. Tomasza. Cross plac Szczepański and turn left into the Planty, passing Pałac Sztuki and its contemporary art cousin Bunkier Sztuki, which has a handily placed sandpit for toddlers outside.

Shopping

CIASTECZKA Z KRAKOWA
www.ciasteczka-z-krakowa.pl
A big range of handmade biscuits, cakes and chocolates are sold in presentation boxes.
🔲 J3 ✉ ul. św. Tomasza 21 ☎ 12 423 2227 🕐 Mon–Sat 9–7, Sun 10–7

CLICK
www.clickfashion.pl
One in a small chain of Polish boutiques, Click sells reasonably priced women's clothes and accessories. The classic styles are strong on color and good for all ages.
🔲 H4 ✉ ul. Grodzka 32 ☎ 12 422 4281 🕐 Mon–Sat 11–8, Sun 12–7

CRACOW POSTER GALLERY
www.cracowpostergallery.com
This is the only gallery in the country specializing in Polish promotional and commercial posters. It organizes special exhibitions and sells more than 2,000 vintage film and exhibition posters by about 100 Polish artists and designers.
🔲 J4 ✉ ul. Stolarska 8–10 ☎ 12 421 2640 🕐 Mon–Fri 11–7, Sat 11–5

DEKOR ART
This eye-pleasing store is crammed to the gills with colorful Polish ceramics bearing simple but beautiful folk designs.
🔲 H3 ✉ ul. Sławkowska ☎ 515 452 969 🕐 Mon–Sat 10–6

DIAMENT
www.diament-jubiler.pl
If you've popped the question in a Krakow carriage and are looking for a ring to seal the deal, this is a good place to come. There's silver and amber of course, but Andrzej Skibiński is also a master goldsmith and will make jewelry to order.
🔲 H4 ✉ ul. Grodzka 62 ☎ 12 422 8707 🕐 Mon–Fri 10–7, Sat–Sun 10–5

GALERIA ORA
www.galeria-ora.com
Come here for a tempting selection of high-quality modern jewelry by local designers who work in silver, amber and a variety of more unusual gemstones.
🔲 H4 ✉ ul. św. Anny 3/1a ☎ 781 661 212 🕐 Mon–Sat 10–8, Sun 11–6

ART AND CRAFT

Robiony ręcznie, meaning "handmade," is a phrase you'll come across a lot in Krakow, especially within the Old Town, where most of the ornaments, glass, jewelry, stained glass, toys and carvings are created by local artisans. The quality is usually high, although whether your loved ones actally want a naïve bird with a golden beak or a rabbit whittled from a single piece of wood only you can tell.

GALERIA OSOBLIWOŚCI
You may not be allowed to take the rhinoceros skull out of the country, but there are plenty of other fascinating things new and old from all over the world in this cabinet of curiosities.
🔲 H3 ✉ ul. Sławkowska 16 ☎ 12 429 1984 🕐 Mon–Fri 11–7, Sat 11–3

GALERIA RYCERSKA
Do you secretly want to be a knight? Here's where to buy your helmet or breastplate—they even have a full suit of hussar's armor.
🔲 J3 ✉ ul. Szpitalna 5 ☎ 601 476 683 🕐 Mon–Fri 11–7, Sat 10–3

KRAKOWSKI KREDENS
www.krakowskikredens.pl
This classy food store devoted to fine local produce, all beautifully packaged, sells biscuits, cakes, preserves, cheeses and more. The cold meat counter is a tribute to Polish ingenuity.
🔲 H4 ✉ ul. Grodzka 7 ☎ 12 423 8159 🕐 Mon–Fri 10–7, Sat 11–7, Sun 11–5

POLSKIE SZKŁO
The shop sells a large selection of traditional and modern Polish glass and crystal, and Christmas decorations year-round.
🔲 H4 ✉ ul. Grodzka 36 ☎ 12 422 5739 🕐 Mon–Fri 10–7, Sat 10–3

Entertainment and Nightlife

CAFÉ PHILO
A very friendly crowd squeeze into this small bar to chat and debate, making it a good place to meet new people.
🚩 J3 ✉ ul. św. Tomasza 30 🕐 Daily 10am–last guest

CLASSICAL MUSIC
There is so much classical music happening in the Old Town that it's difficult to escape the promotional leaflets. Keep your ears peeled for concerts, generally about an hour long, in churches and beautiful rooms in historic buildings. Tickets are usually sold on the door. Timings will vary according to the season but here is a typical selection:

Chopin 🚩 H3 ✉ Pod Gruszką Journalists' Club, ul. Szczepańska 1; Teatru Słowackiego; Pałac Bonerowski 🕾 604 093 570 🕐 Most nights of the week 7pm
Concerts in churches
🚩 H5 ✉ Kościół św. Piotra i Pawła, ul. Grodzka 54 🕾 695 574 526 🕐 Most nights of the week. Organ concerts 5pm, chamber music 8pm
🚩 H5 ✉ Kościół O. O. Bernadynów, ul. Bernardyńska 2 🕾 695 574 526 🕐 Tue, Sat 8.30pm
🚩 H5 ✉ Kościół św. Idziego, ul. Grodzka 67 🕾 695 574 526 🕐 At least 2 nights a week

CRACOW CINEMA CENTER ARS
www.ars.pl
On the site of Kino Sztuka, one of Poland's oldest cinemas, several screens show original-language films—mainly art-house but also the odd blockbuster—with Polish subtitles.
🚩 H3 ✉ ul. św. Jana 6 🕾 12 421 4199; reservations www.dokina.pl 🕐 Daily various times

ENTERTAIN THE DRAGON
www.stawowy.pl
This annual summer season dinner show brings the Krakow cabaret tradition alive for English-speakers.
🚩 H3 ✉ Centrum Sztuki Moliere, ul. Szewska 4 🕾 602 772 265 🕐 Jul–Aug Fri 7pm

FILHARMONIA
www.filharmonia.krakow.pl
One of the largest philharmonic auditoriums in the country hosts a symphonic orchestra, mixed choir and boys' choir. They specialize in large vocal and instrumental

MAVERICK VIRTUOSO
British musician Nigel Kennedy—often called the "punk violinist"—spends much of his time in Krakow, has married a local girl, and likes to work with many of the city's musicians, playing and recording not only with the Filharmonia, but also with jazz and rock artists. Why? "You can be creative with these cats," he says.

works. It also plays in Wawel Castle and the Collegium Novum.
🚩 H4 ✉ Filharmonia im. Karola Szymanowskiego w Krakowie, ul. Zwierzyniecka 1 🕾 12 422 9477, ext. 33, 12 429 1438, ext. 33 🕐 Ticket office Tue–Fri 10–2, 3–7, Sat–Sun 1 hour before the performance 🕭 Free admission for the blind, people with impaired mobility and their companions

JAZZ ROCK CAFÉ
www.jazzrockcafe.pl
People fall into this cellar and never want to leave, intoxicated by the loose atmosphere, wild dancing and rock music.
🚩 H3 ✉ ul. Sławkowska 12 🕾 514 909 907 🕐 Daily 7pm–6am

OPERA KRAKOWSKA
www.opera.krakow.pl
Krakow's opera performs a repertoire of Polish and European classics, in its modern premises near the train station.
🚩 J3 ✉ ul. Lubicz 48 🕾 12 296 6200 🕐 Regular opera seasons, check with ticket office for performance schedule and times

PROZAK
This trendy basement club delivers fresh beats from both local and international DJs to a glitzy crowd over three packed dance floors.
🚩 H4 ✉ plac Dominikański 6 🕾 733 704 650 🕐 Fri–Sat 10pm–8am, Sun–Thu 10pm–6am

Restaurants

PRICES

Prices are approximate, based on a 3-course meal for one person.
€€€ over 170PLN/€50
€€ 100–170PLN/€30–€50
€ under 100PLN/€30

BAR MLECZNY POD TEMIDĄ (€)

www.bar-mleczny.com.pl
By far the best of the many inexpensive dumpling and pancake places in town, this old-fashioned "milk bar" (no alcohol) serves a wide variety of hot, tasty, non-greasy and very fresh Polish food fast.
🚇 H4 ✉ ul. Grodzka 43 ☎ 12 422 0874 🕐 Daily 9–8

CAFÉ CAMELOT (€)

Sample light meals, good salads, celebrated apple cake, all within 13th-century stone walls and on the ground floor.
🚇 H3 ✉ ul. św. Tomasza 17 ☎ 12 421 0123 🕐 Daily 9am–midnight

CAFÉ GOŁĘBIA 3 (€)

Don't post your cards in the blue poczta poetycka postbox outside. It's for your poems. Every week one's fished out and put up in the window.
🚇 H4 ✉ ul. Gołębia 3 ☎ 12 430 2419 🕐 Mon–Sat 9am–11pm, Sun 10am–11pm

CAFÉ LAROUSSE (€)

If the stack of magazines palls, read the walls—it's like sitting in the pages of a 19th-century illustrated book.
🚇 J3 ✉ ul. św. Tomasza 22 🕐 Mon–Sat 9–9, Sun 10–9

CHIMERA (€€)

www.chimera.com.pl
Inventive cooking, using seasonal Polish ingredients—venison, goose, pike-perch, saddle of fallow deer—creates a modern menu.
🚇 H4 ✉ ul. św. Anny 3 ☎ 12 292 1212 🕐 Noon–last guest

CHIMERA SALAD BAR (€)

Next door to its parent (above) but down a passage, this self-service restaurant with hot dishes and a salad bar has become a Krakow institution. It is equally good for romantic students, ladies who lunch and vegetarians. At lunchtime you may have to queue.
🚇 H3 ✉ ul. św. Anny 3 ☎ 12 292 1212 🕐 Noon–last guest

TABLE MANNERS

Smacznego! is Polish for bon appetit! but travelers on a budget need to recognize some other new vocabulary: samo obsługa (self-service) and prosimy o zwrot naczyń (please bring back your empty dishes); places with grander aspirations may advertise that they take rezerwacja stolików (table reservations).

KAWALERIA (€€)

www.kawaleria.com.pl
The award-winning cooking here is accompanied by elegant and well-polished service. The inexpensive lunch menu is available until 4pm.
🚇 H4 ✉ ul. Gołębia 4 ☎ 12 430 2432 🕐 Daily 12–10

METROPOLITAN (€€)

Bored with barszcz and underwhelmed by uszki? Watch the kitchen-stove drama in this smart but not stuffy hotel restaurant as the chefs prepare well-judged contemporary dishes. There is also an interesting wine list.
🚇 H3 ✉ Hotel Saski, ul. Sławkowska 3 ☎ 12 421 9803 🕐 Mon–Sat 7.30am–midnight, Sun 7.30am–10pm

POD GRUSZKĄ (€€)

www.podgruszka.pl
This elegantly appointed, antique-filled restaurant serves a menu of well-executed Polish favorites under heavy chandeliers.
🚇 H3 ✉ ul. Szczepańska ☎ 12 346 5704 🕐 Daily 10am–11pm

U STASI (€)

An authentically utilitarian milk bar, U Stasi plates up all the local favorites but with a menu in English. It's best for lunch between noon and 2pm, after which you'll be eating leftovers.
🚇 J4 ✉ ul. Mikołajska 16 ☎ 12 421 5084 🕐 Mon–Fri 12–5

As the seat of bishops and kings, the limestone outcrop of Wawel Hill was the center of Church and State in Poland from the 11th century until the capital was moved to Warsaw in the late 16th century. The cathedral is still the resting place of Poland's heroes.

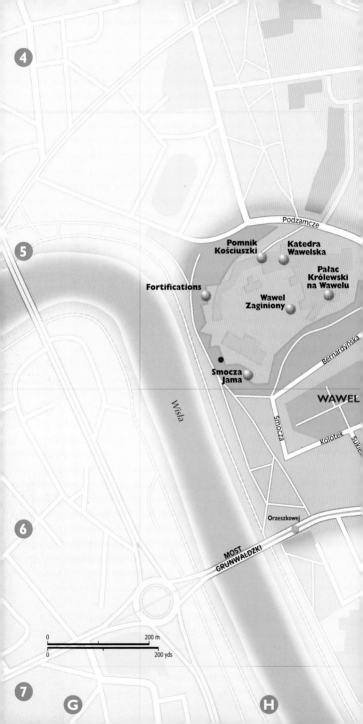

Wawel

Stradomska

Św Agnieszki

Stradom

J DIETLA

J

Katedra Wawelska

As well as being Poland's premier church, Wawel Cathedral has a bell that grants lovers' wishes, heroes in its crypt, the huge silver tomb of Poland's patron saint and the bones of ancient monsters hanging in its doorway.

Bishop's move Krakow's bishops took up residence on Wawel Hill from 1000, and work started on the first cathedral a couple of decades later; a second cathedral was begun in 1085 and consecrated in 1142. Of this, the Romanesque St. Leonard's crypt and a few stones survive. The three-aisle Gothic cathedral we see today was started in 1320 and consecrated in 1364. Most of the chapels, whose domes are so striking as you approach from the gardens, particularly the gold dome of the Renaissance Zygmunt chapel, were added later.

Clockwise from far left: The High Altar; the cathedral's clock tower; the Zygmunt chapel with its golden dome; bell in the Zygmunt tower; sarcophagi in the crypt; St. Stanisław's silver tomb

THE BASICS

www.katedra-wawelska.pl

✚ H5

✉ Wawel 3

☎ 12 429 3327

🕐 Apr–Oct Mon–Sat 9–5, Sun 12.30–5; Nov–Mar Mon–Sat 9–4, Sun 12.30–4; museum Mon–Sat 9–5. Closed holy days and national hols. Last admission an hour before closing

🍴 Cafés on Wawel Hill (€)

♿ Few; lift from Bernardyńska Gate (steep cobbled road accessible by taxi) to garden level and toilets

🎟 Inexpensive

Coronation place The murdered St. Stanisław, former Bishop of Krakow, became a focus for unifying Poland, and his tomb in the cathedral a place of pilgrimage. The kings of Poland chose to be crowned next to his relics and to be buried here, too. The first was Władysław Łokietek ("the Short," called by Poles "the Elbow-high"). Walking around the church, you will see their stone and marble memorials, including that of Queen Jadwiga; their remains are mostly in the crypt below.

Poets and politicians In another part of the crypt are the tombs of the great Polish Romantic poets, Adam Mickiewicz and Juliusz Słowacki. You'll also find the country's heroes: Tadeusz Kościuszko, Marshal Jósef Piłsudski and General Władysław Sikorski, head of the Polish Government in Exile during World War II.

TIP

● If you touch the clapper of the Zygmunt bell with your left hand, they say you will be lucky in love.

Pałac Królewski na Wawelu

HIGHLIGHTS

● Deputies' Hall (Room of Heads)
● Friezes by Hans Dürer (brother of Albrecht) in the Tournament Hall
● The 136 Brussels tapestries
● Collection of 18th-century Meissen porcelain, the coronation service of Augustus III

TIP

● A limited number of tickets is on sale each day. To ensure entry reserve timed tickets in advance for a moderate fee. Call 12 422 1697 or download a form from the website.

Wawel Castle is perhaps Poland's greatest treasure, despite the depredations of invaders who carried off some of its finest pieces. Many of these have been tracked down and returned, and it's all been gleamingly restored—even the furniture polish smells good.

State power The kings of Poland began to live on Wawel Hill from the mid-10th century. King Alexander and his successor Zygmunt the Old commissioned a new palace in the Italian Renaissance style early in the 16th century, its arcaded courtyard decorated with frescoes that visitors can still see today. The last Jagiellonian, Zygmunt II Augustus, added a splendid collection of Brussels tapestries for the Royal Private Apartments, and by the end of the 16th century

Clockwise from far left: Inner courtyard; view of the castle from the river; two of the castle's towers; Coat of Arms Gate; frescoes on the walls of the Renaissance-style courtyard

THE BASICS

www.wawel.krakow.pl

🚇 H5

✉ Wawel 5

☎ 12 422 5155, ext 219

🕐 All tickets are timed. State Rooms Apr–Oct Tue–Fri 9.30–5, Sat–Sun 10–5; Nov–Mar Tue–Sat 9.30–4, Sun 10–4. Royal Private Apartments Apr–Oct Tue–Fri 9.30–5, Sat–Sun 10–5; Nov–Mar Tue–Sat 9.30–4. Crown Treasury and Armory Apr–Oct Mon 9.30–1, Tue–Fri 9.30–5, Sat–Sun 10–5; Nov–Mar Tue–Sat 9.30–4. Sun hours apply 1, 3 May, 15 Aug

🍴 Cafés on Wawel Hill (€)

♿ Few

💰 State Rooms moderate, free Nov–Mar Sun. Royal Private Apartments moderate. Crown Treasury and Armory moderate, free tickets on the day Nov–Mar Mon

❓ There are two ticket offices at Bernardyńska Gate and Herbowa (Coat of Arms Gate). Last admission 1 hour before closing. The arcaded courtyard closes 30 min before the gates to Wawel Hill, which are open from 6am to dusk

Wawel Castle was one of the great cultural centers of Europe. Both the tapestries and the gold coronation sword were taken to safety in Canada before the Nazis occupied the castle; they are back on display today.

Present riches The State Rooms were designed to impress, and still do—it's difficult to drag your eyes down from the carved and painted ceilings. The 30 heads that remain of the original 194 on the ceiling of the Deputies' Hall are so lifelike that you expect them to speak—apart from the one gagged for, as legend has it, telling the king what to do. You must join a small group to see the Royal Private Apartments and the choice paintings from the schools of Titian, Raphael and Botticelli. Don't miss the Oriental Art exhibit either.

Smocza Jama

Bronisław Chromy's statue (left); children examine dragon souvenirs (right)

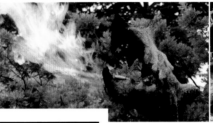

THE BASICS

www.wawel.krakow.pl
- H5
- Wawel Hill
- 12 422 5155,
12 422 6121
- Cave Jul–Aug daily
10–7; May–Jun daily 10–6;
Apr, Sep–Oct daily 10–5
- Cafés on Wawel
Hill (€)
- None for cave, dragon
accessible from coach park
along level river path
- Inexpensive, under-
7s free

HIGHLIGHTS

● Bronisław Chromy's
statue
● The dragon breathes real
flames
● Many fissured limestone
caverns

TIP

● You don't have to buy
a ticket for Wawel Castle
or Cathedral to visit the
Dragon's Lair. Just buy a
separate ticket from the
machine at the top of the
stairs down into the cavern.

**The Smok, or dragon, is the popular
symbol of Krakow, and emblem of the
fire in the belly of this otherwise
intellectual city. You will find its image
everywhere, from green fluffy toys to
jewelry to trade names.**

The legend Long ago in the days when people
first settled in this bend of the Vistula River, King
Krak built his castle on Wawel Hill, little realizing
that underneath him in one of the limestone
caverns there slumbered a dragon. As the peas-
ants took to grazing their sheep and cattle on
the riverbanks, the dragon awoke and began
seizing their livestock, sometimes carrying off
young women, too. The town was terrified and
the king offered his daughter's hand in marriage
and his whole kingdom to whoever could slay
the beast. Knight after knight died fighting the
creature, until a young shoemaker offered to try.
He asked for sheepskins, mutton fat and a great
deal of sulfur. By dawn he had constructed a
fleecy ram, smeared with fat and stuffed with
sulfur. The dragon woke and gobbled up the
baited breakfast. As the sulfurous fire raged in
its stomach, it drank and drank from the river to
try to put it out—until eventually it exploded. So
the cobbler won the princess and the kingdom.

Today You can see the dragon, a spiky statue
by Bronisław Chromy, by following the riverbank
below Wawel Hill, or by climbing down 135
steps from the top of the hill and emerging at
the river through the Dragon's Lair. The fero-
cious beast still emits a fearsome flame.

More to See

FORTIFICATIONS

Looking towards Wawel Hill from the Old Town you see many towers, but not all are defensive. The farthest away, from an Old Town vantage point, are those of the cathedral: the Clock, Zygmunt and Silver Bells towers. Seen from the east, the mainly Renaissance castle retains the Gothic Jordanka, Danish and Kurza Stopka (Hen's Foot) towers and the baroque Zygmunt III corner tower. Farther around the hill toward the river, you'll find three tall brick towers, begun in the 15th century: Baszta Złodzieska or the Thieves' Tower; Baszta Sandomierska; and the Senators' Tower or Lubranka.

🏛 H5 ✉ Wawel Hill ☎ 12 422 5155 ♿ None

POMNIK KOŚCIUSZKIEGO

If you approach Wawel Hill from ul. Kanoniczka, the mounted statue of the soldier and engineer Tadeusz Kościuszko, designed by Leonard Marconi in 1921, can be seen near the Coat of Arms Gate. A Polish freedom fighter, Kościuszko also joined the Americans in their battle for independence and befriended Washington and Jefferson. In 1794 he declared in Krakow the insurrection against the Russians.

🏛 H5 ✉ Wawel Hill ☎ 12 422 5155 🍴 Cafés below the hill (€) ♿ None

WAWEL ZAGINIONY

The Lost Wawel exhibition is an atmospheric and imaginative collection based on the remnants of the Renaissance royal kitchens, what's left of the Gothic royal castle and a 9th-century chapel. It also includes archaeological finds from centuries of excavation. There are diagrams of the different phases of building on Wawel Hill, as well as computer simulations of the more important vanished buildings and a model of the hill in the 18th century.

🏛 H5 ✉ Wawel 5 ☎ 12 422 5155, ext 219 🕐 Apr–Oct Mon 9.30–1, Tue–Fri 9.30–5, Sat–Sun 10–5; Nov–Mar Tue–Sat 9.30–4, Sun 10–4 ♿ None 🎫 Inexpensive, free tickets on the day Apr–Oct Mon; Nov–Mar Sun

Wawel Zaginiony

Equestrian statue of Tadeusz Kościuszko

Restaurants

PRICES

Prices are approximate, based on a 3-course meal for one person.

€€€ over 170PLN/€50
€€ 100–170PLN/
€30–€50
€ under 100PLN/€30

AQUARIUS (€)

www.aquariuskrakow.pl
Board the barge via a 7m (23ft) gangplank for a choice of dining experiences. The formal restaurant downstairs specializes in fish and seafood, while the self-service café on the upper deck offers an international menu. Music enlivens most weekends and children get coloring books to keep them amused.
➕ H5 ✉ Moored by Bulwar Czerwieński (near Jubilat Department Store) ☎ 12 427 2003 🕐 Daily 12–10

GĄDEK (€)

www.piekarnia-gadek.com
A bakery, pastry shop and sweet shop that's been going for more than 60 years, Gądek also serves hot *zapiekanki* or Polish pizzas to take away—ideal for refueling inexpensively or to make a picnic lunch to eat by the Vistula.
➕ H6 ✉ 19 ul. Koletek ☎ 12 422 5553 🕐 Mon–Fri 6am–7pm, Sat 6am–2pm

KAWIARNIA POD BASZTĄ (€)

The Café Under the Tower is perfectly sited for the weary tourist. Right on the hill, it provides a full international menu as well as drinks and snacks. In the summer months, outside tables mean you can eat your ice cream while looking across the gardens at some of Krakow's most beautiful sights.
➕ H5 ✉ 9 Wawel ☎ 12 422 7528 🕐 Apr–Jun, Sep–Oct Mon–Fri 9–5, Sat–Sun 9–6; Nov–Mar daily 9–4; Jul–Aug daily 9–8 ♿ Lift from Bernardyńska Gate (steep cobbled road accessible by taxi) and toilets

POD SMOCZĄ JAMĄ (€)

www.jama.krakow.pl
The dragon painted on the wall is trying to quench the fire with beer, but most of the diners choose from the traditional Polish dishes or wide-ranging international fare on offer.

GO GRILLING

All over Krakow, but particularly near the river, you'll find informal open-air eating places inviting you to barbecue your own meat or sausage. They are a good choice for a basic summer lunch or dinner, usually washed down with beer. Recognize them by the rustic wood decor—tables might be old cable reels and seats tree trunks still clad in bark.

➕ H5 ✉ 24 ul. Podzamcze ☎ 12 422 2921 🕐 Mon–Sat 9–8, Sun 10–8

POD WAWELEM (€)

With its beerhall atmosphere, oompah bands, wood-paneled dining room with long benches, beer garden and liter steins of lager, you'd be excused for thinking this popular place had been brought wholesale on a truck straight from Bavaria. The menu is mostly Polish, though it also offers a host of other dishes from around central Europe to soak up the beer.
➕ H6 ✉ ul. św. Gertrudy 26–29 ☎ 12 421 2336 🕐 Mon–Sat noon–midnight, Sun noon–11

SMAK UKRAIŃSKI (€)

www.ukrainska.pl
Experience the little-known cuisine of Poland's neighbor at this delightfully cozy cellar restaurant. The stone walls are bedecked with traditional Ukrainian embroidery and carpets from the Carpathian Mountains, and the menu includes lots of hearty Slavic comfort food such as borsht, Kiev meatballs, beef goulash with buckwheat, and pancakes. Wash it all down with Crimean and Georgian wines or Obolon beer from Kiev.
➕ H5 ✉ ul. Kanonicza 15 ☎ 12 421 9294 🕐 Daily 12–10

IZaaKA i AMALJI POTOK
DAR

Founded by Kazimierz the Great in 1335, and incorporated into Krakow proper in 1791, Kazimierz today is full of new enterprise. It buzzes with bohemian clubs, shops and cafés, yet at the same time celebrates its rich Jewish history.

4

5

6

7

DIETLA

Wrzesińska

Starowiślna

STAROWIŚLNA

Berka
Joselewicza

Miodowa

DIETLA

**Synagoga i
Cmentarz Remuh**

Miodowa

Warszauera

**Synagoga
Izaaka**

Szeroka

Stradom

Kupa

Izaaka

Ciemna

**Plac
Nowy**

**Synagoga
Wysoka**

**Stara
Synago**

Józefa

**Kościół
Bożego Ciała**

Wawrzyńca

Krakowska

Bożego

Ciała

Św.

**Muzeum
Inżynieri
Miejskiej**

Czarna

**Muzeum
Etnograficzne**

Bocheńska

KAZIMIERZ

Plac
Wolnica

Podgórsk

Kładka
Ojca
Bernat

MOST J
Piłsu Dkiego

0   300 m

0   300 yds

H   **J**

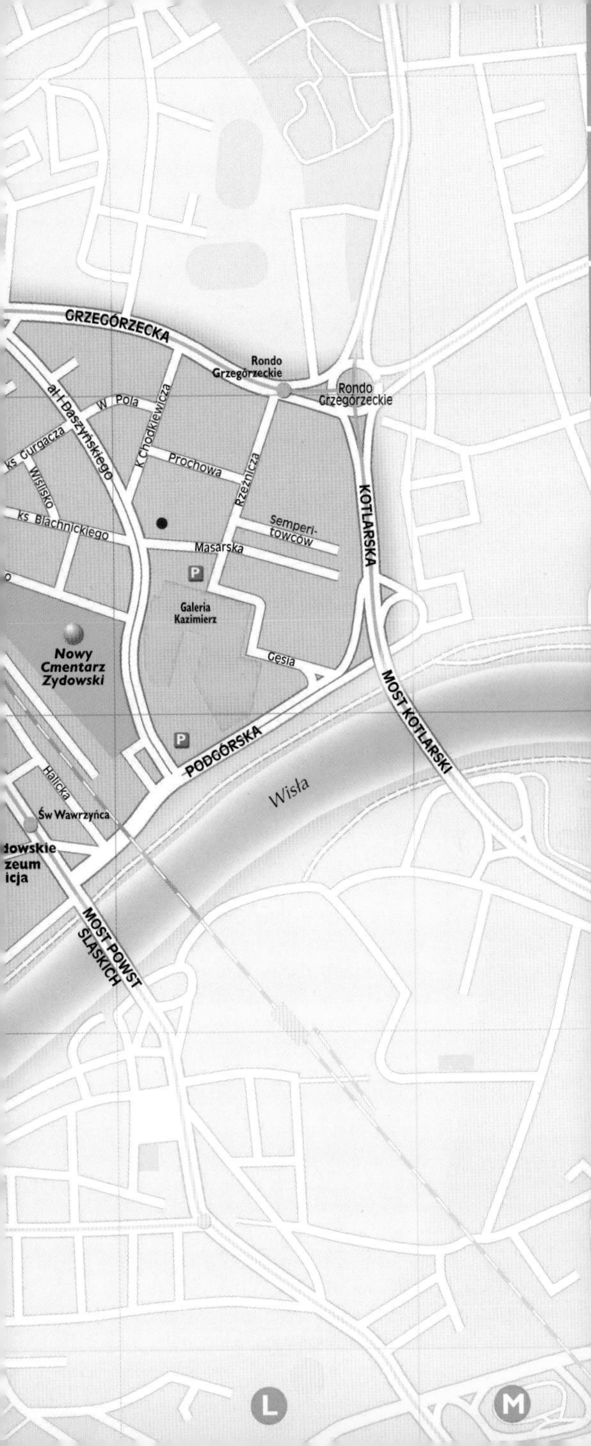

GRZEGÓRZECKA

Rondo
Grzegórzeckie

Rondo
Grzegórzeckie

W. Pola

al.H.Daszyńskiego

ks.Guriacza

K.Chodkiewicza

Prochowa

Wietska

ks.Blachnickiego

Rzeźnicza

Semperi-
towców

Masarska

P

Galeria
Kazimierz

Gęsia

Nowy
Cmentarz
Żydowski

KOTLARSKA

MOST KOTLARSKI

P

PODGÓRSKA

Wisła

Halicka

Św Wawrzyńca

dowskie
zeum
icja

MOST POWST.
ŚLĄSKICH

L

M

Kazimierz

Muzeum Etnograficzne

● Potter's workshop
● Krakowianka costumes
● Traditional Krakow Christmas cribs
● Display showing traditional festivals in the region

DID YOU KNOW?

● The bronze bas-relief on the northern wall showing Kazimierz the Great admitting the Jews to Poland is a version by Henryk Hochman of his 1910 original.

This museum devoted to the traditional life and customs of local people, particularly those in the surrounding countryside, has inhabited the old town hall of Kazimierz for almost 60 years.

Historic location The earliest mention of a town hall in plac Wolnica, the large market square of Kazimierz, was in 1369. The building you see today was built in the 16th century with later additions. It became redundant when Kazimierz was absorbed into Krakow in 1791 and ceased to be a separate town. The Ethnographic Museum moved here just after World War II.

Country lives Drawing its exhibits mainly from the 19th century, and initially the work

of one amateur collector, Seweryn Udzieli, the museum's collection of 80,000 items provides a fascinating glimpse of rural life and customs in Poland as they were until very recently. The interiors of the traditional cottages reconstructed in the museum show how everything, from the baby's crib to the butter churn, was handmade out of the most readily available material—wood. Many of the walls are painted with flower motifs, echoing the colorful embroidery on the folk costumes on display from various regions of Poland. You can compare how custom and habits differed between Małopolska, the region surrounding Krakow, and other parts of Poland. Don't miss the work of folk artists Nikifor Wawry and Józef Janos. The museum also has occasional special exhibitions devoted to other parts of the world.

THE BASICS

www.etnomuzeum.eu

➕ J6

✉ Ratusz, plac Wolnica 1

☎ 12 430 5575

🕐 Tue–Wed, Fri–Sat 11–7, Thu 11–9, Sun 11–3.

🚌 504 to Plac Wolnica. Tram 6, 8, 10, 13 to plac Wolnica

♿ Good, lift and ramp

✋ Inexpensive; special exhibitions also inexpensive

Plac Nowy

TOP 25

Alchemia bar on plac Nowy (left); antiques for sale (right)

THE BASICS

➕ J6

✉ plac Nowy

🕐 Stalls daily 8–4

🍴 Fast food daily 9am–2am (€)

🚃 Tram 3, 9, 19 to ul. Miodowa

♿ Flat but very uneven

HIGHLIGHTS

● A drink in Alchemia (▷ 83)
● A *zapiekanka* (half a baguette pizza-style with toppings) or plate of *placki* (potato pancakes) from Endzior in the green rotunda
● Sunday morning flea market

TIP

● As with any big city market, do watch out for pickpockets.

DID YOU KNOW?

● Plac Nowy is the focus of Krakow's popular Soup Festival each May.

As the center of bohemian Krakow, this is where people come to begin long hedonistic nights, but once it was known as "Jewish Square" and was the hub of a very different kind of life and trade.

Yesterday Something of the old days still hangs around plac Nowy, particularly in the daytime; there's a sense in which it has not fully joined 21st-century Kazimierz. Running along one side of the square, ul. Estery is said to be named for Esther, Kazimierz the Great's Jewish mistress, while nearby ul. Ciemna, or Dark Street, is so named because it had no street lighting until after 1900. This was always the trading square of a district that for a long time was cut off from Krakow by Stara Wiślna or the Old Vistula river, which was only filled in to form ul. Dietla in the late 19th century.

Today The Okrąglak, the green-painted round building in the center of the square, dating from about 1900 and once used as a kosher slaughterhouse, is occupied by vendors of Polish fast food. Their establishments are patronized by local workers and budget travelers, who stand at metal counters to eat, and each has its devotees. Alchemia, the bar and music hall that epitomizes bohemian Kazimierz, stands on one corner, and many other bars and clubs catering for the young and hip have opened in the area. More traditional restaurants with *klezmer* music are found along ul. Szeroka, which caters to tourists.

The bimah (left); the exterior of the Old Synagogue (middle); a prayer hall (right)

Stara Synagoga

The oldest surviving synagogue in Poland, this imposing Renaissance building at the top of Kazimierz's main square is now a museum and a good first stop for finding out about the area's Jewish history.

Florentine accent A synagogue was first erected here in 1407, partly built into the Kazimierz city walls. Today's structure was largely the work of Florentine architect Matteo Gucci in 1570, though he kept the form of the older brick-ribbed vaulting. Later in the 16th and 17th centuries, two women's prayer sections were added, as were other extensions to enable it to serve as both a religious and an administrative center for the Jewish community. In World War II, the chandeliers were taken by the Nazi governor, Hans Frank, and the building used as a warehouse. By the end of 1944 the vaulting had collapsed. It remained in a ruined state until the end of the 1950s, when renovation began to turn it into a museum.

Heritage restored In the wall at the main entrance you'll see a baroque alms box, while inside the main prayer hall the *bimah*, with a wrought-iron canopy over a 12-sided stone base, is a replica of the 16th-century original. The exhibition in the main hall is dedicated to objects related to the important holidays of the Jewish calendar, such as porcelain and silver plates for the Passover bread and *kiddush* cups used on the Sabbath. The most important is a scroll with the text of the Torah.

THE BASICS

www.mhk.pl
* K6
* ul. Szeroka 24
* 12 422 0962
* Apr–Oct Mon 10–2, Tue–Sun 9–5; Nov–Mar Mon 10–2, Tue, Thu, Sat–Sun 9–4, Fri 10–5
* Tram 3, 9, 19 to ul. Miodowa
* None
* Inexpensive, Mon free; English audio guide inexpensive

HIGHLIGHTS

● Menorah
● Late-Renaissance stone Ark
● Collection of drawings and paintings of the streets of old Kazimierz
● Original collecting box for alms
● Reconstructed *bimah* (Torah reader's platform)

Synagoga i Cmentarz Remuh

TOP 25

The Wailing Wall (left); detail of the bimah (middle); gravestones in the cemetery (right)

THE BASICS

www.krakow.jewish.org.pl

K5

ul. Szeroka 40

12 429 5735,
12 430 5411

Sun–Fri 9–6, Sat 9–4
for prayer and services
only

Tram 3, 9, 19 to ul.
Miodowa

None

Inexpensive

HIGHLIGHTS

● Plaque marking
the place where Moses
Isserles prayed
● 17th-century *bimah* door
● Late Renaissance Ark
with inscriptions carved
in 1558
● Renaissance collection box

TIP

● Women should cover
their shoulders and men
their heads. No visitors are
allowed during services.

DID YOU KNOW?

● Traditionally, no one
ever sits in the place where
Moses Isserles prayed. It is
marked by a burning lamp.

Second in age to the Old Synagogue, the Remuh Synagogue is the only one in Krakow where religious services are still held regularly. Despite its small size, it has an important place in Jewish culture.

Holy giant Founded in 1553 by Israel Isserles Auerbach, King Zygmunt August's banker, the synagogue is named after his son, the Talmudic scholar Rabbi Moses Isserles, whose name was shortened to Remuh. Jewish people from all over Europe settled in Kazimierz, bringing different customs with them. The Talmudic Academy, founded by Moses Isserles in 1550, was instrumental in unifying Judaic law for these disparate traditions.

Ancient tombs The rabbi is buried in the cemetery immediately behind the synagogue with the inscription "Between Moses and Moses, nobody arose in Israel to equal Moses." The cemetery, which was closed to burials in 1800, contains some of the oldest tombstones in Poland. When it was restored after the Nazi desecration of World War II, a row of shallowly buried tombstones was discovered. These have been erected to separate the cemetery from ul. Szeroka and are known as the "Wailing Wall."

Continuing tradition Today, the synagogue has been renovated in a simple fashion after it was used for storage during the Nazi occupation and its treasures plundered. It is now run by the Jewish community.

Żydowskie Muzeum Galicja

The museum's book-shop (left); the Traces of Memory exhibition (right)

Set up by the late British photographer Chris Schwarz, the Galicia Jewish Museum aims to shed new light on Jewish history, celebrating the eight centuries of Jewish culture in Poland, while also commemorating those who perished in the Holocaust.

Vanished lives Chris Schwarz was already a successful photographer in London when he moved to Krakow to set up this museum. An inspired and inspiring figure, he regretted the way that the atrocity of the Holocaust had blotted out memories of the rich Jewish heritage in Poland and set about remedying that. On display here you'll find a permanent exhibition called Traces of Memory, consisting of photographs taken by Schwarz with a commentary by social anthropologist Professor Jonathan Webber. The two spent 12 years traveling together documenting the Jewish past in Poland. The result is a completely original body of work.

New vision As well as an excellent and extensive bookshop, the museum has a rich program of events, many in English, in which visitors are welcome to take part. Its main brief is to commission exhibitions and publications about Jewish history and culture and run educational programs, while stimulating interfaith discussion and debate. The net is spread very wide. There might be a film showing in the evening, or perhaps a lecture or a *klezmer* concert.

THE BASICS

www.galiciajewish
museum.org

➕ K6

✉ ul. Dajwór 18

☎ 12 421 6842

🕐 Daily 10–6

🍴 Café (€)

🚊 Tram 1, 3, 9, 11, 12, 19 to ul. Starowiślna/ul. św. Wawrzyna

♿ Excellent

💲 Inexpensive

❓ Many special events and temporary exhibitions. Contact the museum for details

HIGHLIGHTS

● Traces of Memory exhibition
● Bookshop
● *Klezmer* concerts—tickets at moderate prices

More to See

KOŚCIÓŁ BOŻEGO CIAŁA

When Kazimierz the Great chartered the new town, it needed a parish church, so Bożego Ciała (Corpus Christi in English) was begun in 1342. First it was built in brick and wood, then, as building and rebuilding continued, it became greater and grander. By the end of the 16th century it was a huge Gothic basilica, while the rich baroque interior was added in the 17th and 18th centuries.

➕ J6 ✉ ul. Bożego Ciała 26 ☎ 12 430 6290; 12 430 6294 🕐 Daily, services 6.30am–7pm 🚋 Tram 6, 8, 10, 13 to plac Wolnica ♿ None 🎟 Free

MUZEUM INŻYNIERII MIEJSKIEJ

www.mimk.com.pl

If your taste runs to old machinery rather than old churches, the Museum of Urban Engineering might appeal. There's a permanent exhibition of old motorbikes and cars, mainly Polish-made, as well as a collection of public transportation vehicles from decades gone by.

There's also an interactive scientific area for children aged five to nine, with lots of ropes and switches to push and pull, where many but not all the explanations are in English. It's housed in the former Krakow tram depot and bus garage.

➕ K6 ✉ ul. św. Wawrzyńca 15 ☎ 12 421 1242 🕐 Jun–Sep Tue, Thu, Sun 10–6, Wed, Fri–Sat 10–4; Oct–May Tue–Sun 10–4 🍴 Brasserie café/restaurant (€) 🚋 Tram 6, 8, 10, 13 to plac Wolnica ♿ Good 🎟 Inexpensive

NOWY CMENTARZ ŻYDOWSKI

The New Jewish Cemetery opened in 1800 when the Remuh cemetery no longer had space. It is the resting place of many eminent Jewish people of Krakow, from rabbis to painters, professors and politicians. Just inside the entrance there is a memorial to those who died in the Holocaust.

➕ K5 ✉ ul. Miodowa 55 🕐 Sun–Fri 8–6. Closed Jewish holidays 🚋 Tram 3, 9, 19, 24 to ul. Miodowa ♿ None 🎟 Free ❓ Men must cover their heads to enter

Corpus Christi Church

Tombstones in the New Jewish Cemetery

SYNAGOGA IZAAKA

According to legend, the largest of Kazimierz's synagogues was built in 1644, after its founder, Izaak Jacubowicz, found treasure. Tuscan columns supporting the women's gallery are indicative of its early baroque style. The stuccoed cradle vault is the largest in Krakow and there are still traces of 17th- and 18th-century wall paintings. After wartime desecration, the relatively recent renovation continues.

➕ K6 ✉ ul. Kupa 18 ☎ 12 430 5577 🕙 Sun–Fri 9–7 🚋 Tram 3, 9, 19, 24 to ul. Miodowa ♿ None 💷 Inexpensive

SYNAGOGA TEMPEL

www.krakow.jewish.org.pl

This was built in the 1860s as a progressive synagogue. Inside you'll find a riot of well-restored color, stained glass, gilt and ornament with Sephardic influences, in contrast to the white walls of older synagogues in the area.

➕ J5 ✉ ul. Miodowa 23–24 ☎ 12 429 5411 🕙 Sun–Fri 10–6. Closed Jewish holidays 🚋 Tram 3, 9, 19, 24 to ul. Miodowa ♿ None 💷 Inexpensive ❓ Female visitors should cover shoulders, men their heads

SYNAGOGA WYSOKA

www.krakow.jewish.org.pl

The late 16th-century High Synagogue was so named because the prayer hall is on the second floor—originally there were shops below. In design, it has much in common with Prague's High Synagogue, underlining the close ties between the two cities in that period. Today it has a large, well-stocked bookshop.

➕ K6 ✉ ul. Józefa 38 🚋 Tram 3, 9, 19, 24 to ul. Miodowa ♿ None 💷 Inexpensive

ULICA SZEROKA

Ul. Szeroka is what remains of the main square of the old village of Bawjół, said to be the first site of the Krakow Academy, the forerunner of the Jagiellonian University.

➕ K5 ✉ ul. Szeroka 🍴 Many restaurants and cafés 🚋 Tram 3, 9, 19, 24 to ul. Miodowa

Bookshop in Synagoga Wysoka

Café on ul. Szeroka

Jewish Heritage Trail

Winding back and forth through the streets of Kazimierz between the Jewish landmarks, you'll see how the area is changing fast.

DISTANCE: 3.5km (2 miles) **ALLOW:** 2–3 hours

START

STARA SYNAGOGA
✚ K6 🚊 Tram 3, 13, 24 to ul. Miodowa

❶ Walking down ul. Szeroka, Remuh Synagogue (▷ 76) and the cemetery's "Wailing Wall" are on your left. Roughly opposite is the Popper Synagogue, now a youth center. At the end on the right, Klezmer Hois is where the ritual baths once stood.

❷ Take the path by Klezmer Hois, turn right down ul. Miodowa, cross ul. Starowislśna (watch out for the trams), and go straight on under the railway bridge to the New Jewish Cemetery (▷ 78) on your left.

❸ Retrace your steps, turning left on to ul. Starowislśna, cross and make your way down ul. Dajwór on your right. Here you'll find the Galicia Jewish Museum (▷ 77).

❹ At the end of the road turn right on to ul. św. Wawrzyńca. The Museum of Urban Engineering (▷ 78) is halfway down on your left.

END

PLAC WOLNICA
✚ J6 🚊 Tram 6, 8, to ul. Krakowska

❾ Leaving the church, turn right down ul. św. Wawrzyńca towards Plac Wolnica. Here you'll find the Ethnographic Museum (▷ 72–73).

❽ Continuing down ul. Miodowa away from the Kupa Synagogue, turn left down ul. Bożego Ciała to the church for which it is named (▷ 78).

❼ Walk back to the corner of ul. Miodowa and ul. Podbrzezie to the Tempel Synagogue (▷ 79, pictured left).

❻ Continue to the top of ul. Kupa. The 1640s Kupa Synagogue is on your right.

❺ Cross back up ul. Wąska to ul. Józefa, where you'll find the High Synagogue (▷ 79). Turn right up ul. Kupa to the Izaak Synagogue (▷ 79).

KAZIMIERZ WALK

Shopping

ANTYKI JÓZEFA
Antiques shops in Krakow tend to be either very high-class (and pricey) or full of junk. This treads the middle ground, with tableware and ornaments as well as furniture.
🔢 J6 ✉ ul. Kupa 3 ☎ 12 422 0127 🕐 Mon–Fri 10.30–6, Sat 10.30–2

AUSTERIA
www.austeria.pl
Krakow's largest Jewish bookstore is in the High Synagogue and is the best place to source book's on the region's Jewish past.
🔢 K6 ✉ ul. Józefa 38 ☎ 12 430 6889 🕐 Sun–Thu 10–6, Fri–Sat 10–7

BLAZKO KINDERY
www.blazko.pl
It calls itself a jewelry art gallery and does not overstate the case. It sells lots of good-quality pieces from contemporary designers, mainly in acrylic and silver.
🔢 J6 ✉ ul. Józefa 11 ☎ 508 646 298 🕐 Mon–Fri 11–6, Sat–Sun 11–5

GALERIA KAZIMIERZ
www.galeriakazimierz.pl
This air-conditioned mall has 130 shops, restaurants and cafés.
🔢 L5 ✉ ul. Podgórska 34, near Most Kotlarski ☎ 12 433 0101 🕐 Daily 10–10

GALERIA OLYMPIA
www.olympiagaleria.pl
This commercial art gallery has a varied program of exhibitions by contemporary painters, photographers and sculptors.
🔢 J6 ✉ ul. Józefa 18 ☎ 603 223 008 🕐 Tue–Fri 11–5, Sat 11–2

GALERIA SZALOM
There's nothing hard-edged in this contemporary art gallery, with a selection of quirky, sometimes whimsical paintings and sculptures.
🔢 J6 ✉ ul. Józefa 16 ☎ 12 290 3270 🕐 Mon–Fri 11–6, Sat 11–3

GALERIE D'ART NAÏF
If your appetite for this kind of art has

BUDGET BUYS

Plac Nowy's market is the best value in Kazimierz. The food outlets in the green rotunda dish up huge plates of Polish staples for tiny prices—Endzior is the most celebrated. A *zapiekanka* is half a long baguette with hot, pizza-type topping, while a portion of *placki* (potato pancakes) would feed a family. There are fruit and vegetable stalls daily, as well as antiques and general junk on Saturdays and clothing on Sundays. There's also a Sunday morning flea market at plac pod Halą Targową in the nearby district of Grzegórzki.

been whetted in the Sukiennice, this gallery is where you'll find the real thing. The owner, Leszek Macak, is one of Poland's greatest specialists in the field.
🔢 J6 ✉ ul. Józefa 11 ☎ 12 421 0637 🕐 Mon–Fri 11–5, Sat–Sun 11–3

LU'LUA
www.lulua.pl
This luxurious perfumery has a carefully edited selection of more than 20 exclusive world brands, among them Trumper's cologne for the men and Annick Goutal for the ladies.
🔢 J6 ✉ ul. Józefa 22 ☎ 12 430 0275 🕐 Mon–Fri 11–7, Sat 11–6

PRODUKTY BENEDYKTYŃSKIE
Just across from plac Wolnica, this is the place to buy goods produced by Benedictine monks. There are all sorts of cheese, meat, honey, tea, juice and wine.
🔢 J6 ✉ ul. Krakowska 29 ☎ 12 422 0216 🕐 Mon–Fri 9–6, Sat 9–2

RYTTER
www.rytter.krakow.pl
Enchantingly old-fashioned, this store specializes in old prints and engravings of bygone Krakow. The store even operates its own traditional printing press.
🔢 J5 ✉ ul. św. Gertrudy ☎ 514 303 305 🕐 Mon–Fri 11–6

Entertainment and Nightlife

ALCHEMIA
www.alchemia.com.pl
The freewheeling, guttering-candle, bohemian ambience here sums up the best of Kazimierz nightlife. Who else would schedule a "Peculiar Music Night"? Reservations are recommended for concerts, movies and gigs in the Music Hall.
➕ J6 ✉ ul. Estery 5
☎ 12 421 2200 🕐 Daily 9am–4/5am

B-SIDE
An out-and-out music club for those who love indie rock, indie pop, electroclash and more in a similar vein.
➕ J6 ✉ ul. Estery 16
☎ 694 461 403 🕐 Daily 4pm–midnight

JUDAICA FOUNDATION
www.judaica.pl
It's not all klubbing and *klezmer* in Kazimierz. At the Centre for Jewish Culture you'll find debates, literary events and regular concerts of all kinds of classical music and jazz.
➕ J6 ✉ ul. Meiselsa 17 ☎ 12 430 6449
🕐 Changing program, see leaflets or website for details

KLUB PIĘKNY PIES
The latest incarnation of this long-established, itinerant club is a large Kazimierz joint attracting ex-pats, budget travelers, local artists and pub philosophers. Indie and rock dominate the playlist.
➕ J6 ✉ ul. Bożego Ciała
🕐 Sun–Thu 4pm–3am, Fri–Sat 4pm–5am

KOLETKTYW DAJWÓR
This club, café and booze complex in a Kazimierz courtyard has several venues satisfying a range of musical tastes. Parties go on long into the early hours here and things can get a bit wild.
➕ K6 ✉ ul. Dajwór 16
🕐 Daily 1pm–7am

MŁYNEK CAFÉ
On the edge of the Kazimierz nightlife vortex, this much-recommended vegetarian café-bar has a program of poetry readings and art shows.

KLEZMER MUSIC
Witness a table of young London sophisticates next to an Irish priest and his elderly parishioners all whooping it up to the wild *klezmer* music in a Kazimierz restaurant, and you'll appreciate why *klezmer* is having such a revival. No one can resist the infectious tunes and the wonderful musicianship of those who play this traditional Jewish music. If it's new to you, pick one of the places that offers a *klezmer* band with the evening meal, and enjoy the experience.

➕ J6 ✉ Plac Wolnica 7
☎ 12 430 6202 🕐 Mon–Fri 9–8, Sat 9–4, Sun 2–8

PTASZYŁ
This cozy but elegant restaurant and bar is hung with lots to interest the eye, not just the little fantastical birds that give it its name. The ambience is friendly and arty.
➕ K6 ✉ ul. Szeroka 10
☎ 509 987 102 🕐 Daily 8.30am–last guest

PUB PROPAGANDA
www.pubpropaganda.pl
Communist knickknacks and portraits of Lenin make up the ironic decor in this cult club.
➕ K5 ✉ ul. Miodowa 20
☎ 12 292 0402, 600 331 922
🕐 Daily noon–last guest

SINGER
As the place that first thought of Kazimierz's lace-and-old-sewing-machine decor, Singer has a lot to answer for, but it's still a popular place to while away a lazy day or evening.
➕ J6 ✉ ul. Estery 20/ul. Izaaka 1 ☎ 12 292 0622
🕐 9am–last guest

STAJNIA
www.pubstajnia.pl
If you're on a Schindler quest, this bar's courtyard was used in the film. For the rest of you, it's an air-conditioned party bar and restaurant playing 1980s and Latin music.
➕ J6 ✉ ul. Józefa 12 ☎ 12 423 7202

Restaurants

ARKA NOEGO (€)

www.arkanoegorestauracja.pl
Come here for evening *klezmer* music and good Jewish food.
🔠 K6 ✉ ul. Dajwór 2 ☎ 12 429 1528 🕐 Jul–Aug daily 9am–2am, Sep–Sun daily 10.30am–midnight 🚊 Tram to ul. Miodowa

AWIW (€)

www.awiw.pl
This Jewish pub-restaurant serves inexpensive Polish and Jewish dishes in an intimate vaulted dining room.
🔠 K6 ✉ ul. Szeroka 13 ☎ 519 075 540 🕐 Daily 10–10 🚊 Tram to ul. Miodowa

BOMBAJ TANDOORI (€)

This is just the place if you're yearning for your favorite Indian food.
🔠 K6 ✉ ul. Szeroka 7–8 ☎ 12 422 3797 🕐 Daily 11am–midnight 🚊 Tram to ul. Miodowa

GOŚCINIEC POD ZAMKIEM (€)

www.gosciniec.krakow.pl
Try wild boar steaks or duck in plum brandy sauce in this friendly place, which has free cabaret-theater some evenings in the *piwnica*.
🔠 J5 ✉ ul. Stradomska 11 ☎ 12 292 2212 🕐 Daily 10am–last customer

HORAI (€€)

www.horairestaurant.pl
Pan-Asian Horai serves Japanese sushi, noodles and tempura, Cantonese and Thai dishes.
🔠 J6 ✉ Plac Wolnica 9 ☎ 12 430 0358 🕐 Sun–Thu 12–10, Fri–Sat 12–11 🚊 Tram to plac Wolnica

KLEZMER-HOIS (€)

www.klezmer.pl
Straightforward Jewish-style food is on the menu in one of the first and jolliest of the *klezmer* restaurants, but this isn't the place if you don't like big groups. There's music nightly and reservations are necessary.
🔠 K6 ✉ ul. Szeroka 6 ☎ 12 411 1245 🕐 Daily 9am–10pm 🚊 Tram to ul. Miodowa

KUCHNIA U DOROTY (€)

Tasty, plain Polish cooking makes this is a good place for refueling.
🔠 J6 ✉ ul. Augustiańska 4 ☎ 517 945 338 🕐 Daily 10–9 🚊 Tram to plac Wolnica

NOVA KROVA (€)

www.novakrova.com.pl
Meat-free burgers packed with nutritious ingredients are the main draw at this vegetarian eatery.
🔠 J6 ✉ plac Wolnica 3 ☎ 530 305 304 🕐 Mon–Thu 12–9, Fri–Sat 12–11, Sun 10–9 🚊 Tram to plac Wolnica

ONCE UPON A TIME IN KAZIMIERZ (€)

www.dawnotemu.
nakazimierzu.pl
One of the sights of the area, with a frontage of mocked-up old Kazimierz shops, this is more about the atmosphere than the food. It takes the local obsession with lace tablecloths to new heights.
🔠 K6 ✉ ul. Szeroka ☎ 12 421 2117 🕐 Daily 10am–10.30pm 🚊 Tram to ul. Miodowa

RUBINSTEIN (€€)

www.hotelrubinstein.com
Cosmetics millionairess Helena Rubinstein was born in this house. The menu offers classic international fare and the service from the English-speaking staff is friendly.
🔠 K6 ✉ ul. Szeroka 12 ☎ 12 384 0000 🕐 Mon–Thu 12–10, Fri–Sun 12–11 🚊 Tram to ul. Miodowa

When there's so much to see in the Old Town and Kazimierz it's tempting not to wander beyond the Planty, but you'll find a variety of sights within walking distance outside the heart of the city.

Muzeum Dom Mehoffera

The house of the Modernist artist Józef Mehoffer, restored to how it was when he lived there, gives an insight into the life of one of the leading lights of the Young Poland movement.

Acclaimed artist Coming to prominence at the turn of the 20th century, Mehoffer founded the art group Sztuka with several other leading fin-de-siècle painters. An art figure on the European stage—he designed stained glass for Fribourg cathedral in Switzerland—he was an admired rector of Krakow's Academy of Fine Arts and contributed to the influential arts journals of the day.

Home and studio Already well established as a painter, printmaker, artist in stained glass and interior designer by the time he bought the house in 1930, Mehoffer lived and worked

Clockwise from far left: The drawing room; view of the garden from the house; the house seen from the back garden; painting of Krakow's Market Square by Józef Mehoffer in 1903; butterfly curtains—a replica of Mehoffer's original design; detail of Mehoffer's stained glass

here until he died in 1946, nurturing his garden and entertaining his fellow artists and intellectuals in the Young Poland movement.

Creative life Visiting the house, you begin to get an idea of just how flourishing Krakow was between the wars. Mehoffer was a collector as well as an artist. Like Feliks "Manggha" Jasieński, he enjoyed Japanese art, but he also admired and collected Chinese and Breton ceramics, Jewish art, fine furniture and tapestries, though, sadly, many of his belongings were seized by the Nazis.

The many portraits on the walls show the other main players in Krakow's artistic milieu at the time, such as Jan Matejko, who collaborated with Mehoffer and Wyspiański on renovations to St. Mary's Church at the end of the 19th century, and who would have dined, debated and enjoyed Mehoffer's hospitality here.

THE BASICS

www.mnk.pl

✛ G3

✉ ul. Krupnicza 26

☎ 12 421 1143, 12 423 2079

🕐 Tue–Sun 10–4

♿ None

💰 Inexpensive

Muzeum Narodowe w Krakowie

HIGHLIGHTS

● Wyspiański's designs for stained glass in Wawel Cathedral
● Krakow stained glass from the 13th, 14th and 15th centuries
● *Nike of the Legions* by Jacek Malczewski
● 10th-century silver Włocławek goblet
● 17th-century Persian belt

TIP

● Buy a combined ticket to see all three permanent exhibitions for little more than the price of two.

The top floor of the main building of the National Museum in Krakow has the largest collection of 20th-century Polish art in the city, drawing together all the big names you'll find mentioned on your visits to the main sights.

Century of the new The 20th century was a period of great change in Poland. After independence in 1920, there was a new mood of confidence. Building on the earlier work of the Modernist artists, such as Witkiewicz (or Witkacy), a philosopher, novelist, playwright and visual artist, 20th-century artists engaged with thinkers from beyond their own country and expressed new ideas with vigor. Most of the permanent exhibition, which is taken up with art made after 1945, shows a revival of the struggle for independence, with some interesting

Clockwise from far left: The facade of the National Museum; Wyspiański's Polonia, *a cartoon for a stained-glass window in the cathedral; Jacek Malczewski's* Following the Angel; *the Włocławek goblet*

pieces by, among others, Tadeusz Kantor, the world-famous Krakow artist and playwright.

Domestic arts One floor below the modern art collection, a display of decorative arts and crafts spans the millennium from the early Middle Ages onward, with beautiful early pieces of silverware, stained glass and embroidery, mainly from local churches. Nearer to the present time are examples of 20th-century Polish crafts showing the distinctive traditional styles.

Objects of war The ground-floor exhibition Weapons and Colors in Poland presents another great contrast, with military hardware from the Middle Ages to World War II. Exhibits include a wide variety of arms, armor and the uniforms of Polish military units from the 18th century onward.

THE BASICS

www.mnk.pl

✚ F4

✉ 1 al. 3 Maja

☎ 012 295 5500

🕐 Tue–Sat 10–6, Sun 10–4

🍽 Café (€)

🚌 109, 124, 134, 144, 152. Tram 20

♿ Very good, elevators, ramps and wheelchair hoists

💷 Inexpensive; Sun permanent exhibitions free

Schindler's Krakow

HIGHLIGHTS

● Apteka Pod Orłem
● Memorial in plac Bohaterów Getta—the empty chairs symbolize the ghetto after the liquidation
● Ghetto walls
● Schindler's Emalia factory

DID YOU KNOW?

● Spielberg's movie was based on the novel *Schindler's Ark* by Thomas Keneally.

TIP

● There's a useful plan of the immediate area on the corner outside the Apteka Pod Orłem.

The events in Steven Spielberg's Oscar-winning movie *Schindler's List*, based on the true story of a factory owner who saved more than 1,000 Jews from the Nazis, happened here, in Podgórze.

The ghetto In 1941, the occupying Nazis forced Krakow's 20,000 or so remaining Jews into just 320 buildings in a new ghetto in Podgórze. Forced labor and overcrowding soon took their toll. Deportations to the death camps began in 1942, and in 1943 the ghetto was liquidated, its remaining inhabitants murdered in the streets. You can see the remains of ghetto walls on ul. Lwowska and ul. Limanowskiego across the Powstańców Śląskich bridge from Kazimierz.

The pharmacy One Christian business remained in the ghetto. The pharmacy Apteka

Clockwise from far left: Empty chair sculptures on plac Bohaterów Getta; view of the Nazi labor camp at Płaszów; memorial at Płaszów; exhibition at the Pharmacy under the Eagles; the original ghetto walls

Pod Orłem, Pharmacy under the Eagles, was run by Tadeusz Pankiewicz, who actively helped Jews resist and escape the Nazis. Today it houses a small exhibition on life and death in the ghetto. It also shows films and photographs of prewar life, when Jews made up a quarter of the population of Krakow.

The factory owner Oskar Schindler negotiated for Jews who would otherwise have been taken to the nearby camp at Płaszów to work in his enamel factory. By later transferring his factory to the Sudetenland he managed to rescue more than 1,000 Jewish men and women from certain death. Today, you can see the outside of Schindler's former Emalia factory at ul. Lipowa 4 (down ul. Kącik and under the railway). Now part of the Krakow History Museum, it houses an exhibition on the Nazi occupation of 1939–45.

THE BASICS

www.mhk.pl

Apteka Pod Orłem

🚇 L7

✉ plac Bohaterów Getta 18

☎ 12 656 5625

🕐 Mon 10–2, Tue–Sun 9–5

🚊 Tram 3, 9, 19 to plac Bohaterów Getta

♿ Good

💲 Inexpensive, Mon free; audio guide inexpensive

Schindler's Factory

www.mhk.pl

🚇 M7

✉ ul. Lipowa 4

☎ 12 257 1017

🕐 Apr–Oct Mon 10–4, Tue–Sun 10–8; Nov–Mar Mon 10–2, Tue–Sun 10–6

🚊 Tram 7, 11, 20 to Zabłocie

💲 Inexpensive

More to See

BŁONIA

When the celebration is too great to be contained in Rynek Główny, Cracovians take to the great 48ha (120-acre) Błonia meadow. Used to graze cattle in medieval times, it was the site of grand military parades from the 19th century, and where Poland's first football match was held in 1894. More recently, Pope John Paul II said Mass and canonized saints here several times. It's also a good place to kick a ball or fly a kite and the adjacent Park Jordana has a children's playground. ✚ D4 ✉ Between al. 3 Maja and ul. Reymonta 🚌 109, 124, 134, 144 to Cracovia Hotel. Tram 20 to Cracovia Hotel

KOŚCIÓŁ ŚW. KATARZYNY

Fire, flood and earthquakes have rocked St. Catherine's church since it was founded by Kazimierz the Great in the 14th century. A good example of Krakow Gothic, its interior is a gallery of styles down the ages, including early baroque altars, a 15th-century statue of the Virgin Mary and 15th-century murals in the adjoining cloisters. ✚ J6 ✉ ul. Augustiańska 7 ☎ 12 430 6242 🕐 Daily, first service 6am, last 7pm 🚋 Tram 6, 8, 10, 13 to plac Wolnica ✋ Free

KOŚCIÓŁ PAULINÓW NA SKAŁCE

www.skalka.paulini.pl

The steps of the Church on the Rock are where St. Stanisław was murdered in 1079, allegedly for clashing with the king, Bolesław the Bold. St. Stanisław's statue outside the baroque church overlooks a pool of holy water into which the saint's severed finger fell. Eminent Poles, including writer and painter Wyspiański, the composer Syzmanowski and the Nobel Prizewinning poet Czesław Miłosz, are buried in the crypt. ✚ H6 ✉ ul. Skałeczna 15 ☎ 12 421 7244 🕐 Church and crypt Apr–Oct Mon–Sat 9–12, 1–5, Sun 10–12, 1–5; other times by appointment 🚋 Tram 6, 8, 10, 13 to plac Wolnica ✋ Free

Muzeum Sztuki i Techniki Japońskiej Manggha

MUZEUM SZTUKI I TECHNIKI JAPOŃSKIEJ MANGGHA

www.manggha.krakow.pl

Named for Feliks "Manggha" Jasieński and founded by the movie director Andrzej Wajda to display the connoisseur's collection of Japanese art, the Museum of Japanese Art and Technology Manggha is a striking piece of contemporary architecture by the Vistula. It has a splendid collection of Japanese woodcuts, handicrafts, weaponry and porcelain, as well as a good sushi restaurant, and also hosts temporary exhibitions.

🔲 G6 ✉ ul. Konopnickiej 26 ☎ 12 267 2703, 12 267 3753 ⏱ Tue–Sun 10–6 🍴 Restaurant (€) 🚊 Tram 1, 2, 6 to Jubilat/Most Dębnicki ♿ Excellent 💷 Moderate

OGRÓD BOTANICZNY

www.ogrod.uj.edu.pl

The Jagiellonian University's Botanical Gardens are Poland's oldest and largest, first laid out in 1783. Though not extensive, they are a relaxing haven 15 minutes' walk from the city center. Investigate the Palmaiarna greenhouse wrapped around a group of palms several floors high—stairs take you level with the treetops.

🔲 L3 ✉ ul. Mikołaja Kopernika 27 ☎ 12 663 3624 ⏱ Daily 9–7 (winter 9–5); glasshouses Tue–Sun 10–4. Botanical museum currently closed for renovation ♿ Good 💷 Inexpensive

ULICA POMORSKA

www.mhk.pl

This plain, former student residence was used by the Gestapo during World War II as a center for detention and torture. The cells are preserved, and there is also a very good permanent exhibition on Krakow 1939–56 with photographs and memorabilia of the resistance. The place has a powerful atmosphere.

🔲 G2 ✉ ul. Pomorska 2 ☎ 12 633 1414 ⏱ Apr–Oct Tue–Sat 10–5.30; Nov–Mar Tue–Wed, Fri 9–4, Thu 12–7, Sat–Sun 10–5 🚊 Tram 4, 8, 13, 14 to plac Inwalidów 💷 Inexpensive

The crypt inside the Church on the Rock

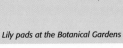

Lily pads at the Botanical Gardens

Restaurants

PRICES

Prices are approximate, based on a 3-course meal for one person.
€€€ over 170PLN/€50
€€ 100–170PLN/ €30–€50
€ under 100PLN/€30

BAL (€)

A great stop-off after visiting Schindler's Factory, this stylishly utilitarian breakfast, brunch and lunch place has minimalist decor, a blackboard menu and a clientele of clutter-hating design types. The menu includes soup, quiche, sandwiches and coffee, providing a respite from the medieval meat-and-kitsch of the Old Town eating scene.
✚ M6 ✉ ul. Ślusarska 9 ☎ 604 814 484 🕙 Mon–Sat 8.30am–10pm, Sun 8.30am–9pm

CAFÉ SZAFÉ (€)

www.cafeszafe.com
A bright, cozy, quirkily decorated café, this also hosts music, stand-up and all sorts of arts events. It's a popular expat hangout. You can get good coffee and cake, too.
✚ G4 ✉ ul. Felicjanek 10 ☎ 663 905 652 🕙 Mon–Fri 9am–1am, Sat–Sun 10am–midnight

CHATA (€)

www.polskakuchnia.com.pl
Better-than-average Polish dishes are served in the standard rustic interior with wooden beams and brick walls. The menu also offers big "feasts"—a selection of dishes for several people to share.
✚ H2 ✉ ul. Krowoderska 21 ☎ 888 101 100 🕙 Daily 1–11

DYNIA (€)

www.dynia.krakow.pl
You get a warm welcome from the hip and friendly young staff in this brick-walled restaurant, with a courtyard for outdoor eating in summer. Come for breakfast, sandwiches, lots of grills and a carefully calorie-counted "fitness menu" too. The

REALITY CHECK

The stalls at Stary Kleparz, though scarcely a couple of minutes' walk beyond the Planty, are a world away from the tourist-pleasing wares of the Sukiennice. Here are huge pants and nasty cardigans, stalls full of old-fashioned alarm clocks or seedlings ready to plant out in your veg patch. But there's also good bread, sausages and cheese, so it's the ideal place to assemble a picnic lunch. Good buys are local honey and strings threaded with dried wild mushrooms.
✚ H2 ✉ ul. Krowoderska 22 ☎ 12 634 1532, www.starykleparz.com 🕙 Mon–Sat 7–7

kitchen closes an hour before the bar.
✚ J3 ✉ ul. Krupnicza 20 ☎ 12 430 0838 🕙 Mon–Fri 8am–11pm, Sat–Sun 9am–11pm

INDALO CAFÉ (€)

www.cafeindalo.pl
This arts and crafts gallery-cum-giftshop with a hippyish feel also serves snacks, coffee, beer and wine.
✚ H5 ✉ ul. Tarłowska 15 ☎ 12 431 0091 🕙 Mon–Sat 9am–10pm, Sun 10–10

PIZZA FRESCO (€)

www.pizzafresco.com.pl
This romantically decorated "piano restaurant" next to the Hotel Niebieski has a small garden for outside dining in summer. The menu is a pizza-pasta Italian combo with a few local touches, such as apple strudel and cheesecake.
✚ F6 ✉ ul. Flisacka 3 ☎ 12 297 4040 🕙 Mon–Sat 12–10, Sun 12–9. Piano concerts Wed–Sat from 7.30pm

PLAŻA KRAKÓW (€€)

www.plazakrakow.com.pl
Most visitors don't come to Krakow to work up a tan on a beach, but the large Krakow Beach complex on the Vistula to the south of Kazimierz has a stretch of sand, a nightclub and this sassy, modern restaurant.
✚ H7 ✉ ul. Ludwinowska 2 ☎ 530 950 303 🕙 Daily 11–11

Farther Afield

If you only have a couple of days in Krakow, you may choose to make one of these trips with a tour company, but they are all easy to reach by public transport and any one will add a different dimension to your visit to the city.

Wolbrom

Miechów

Wyżyna Krakowsko-Częstochowska

E77

Skała

Słomniki

Farther Afield

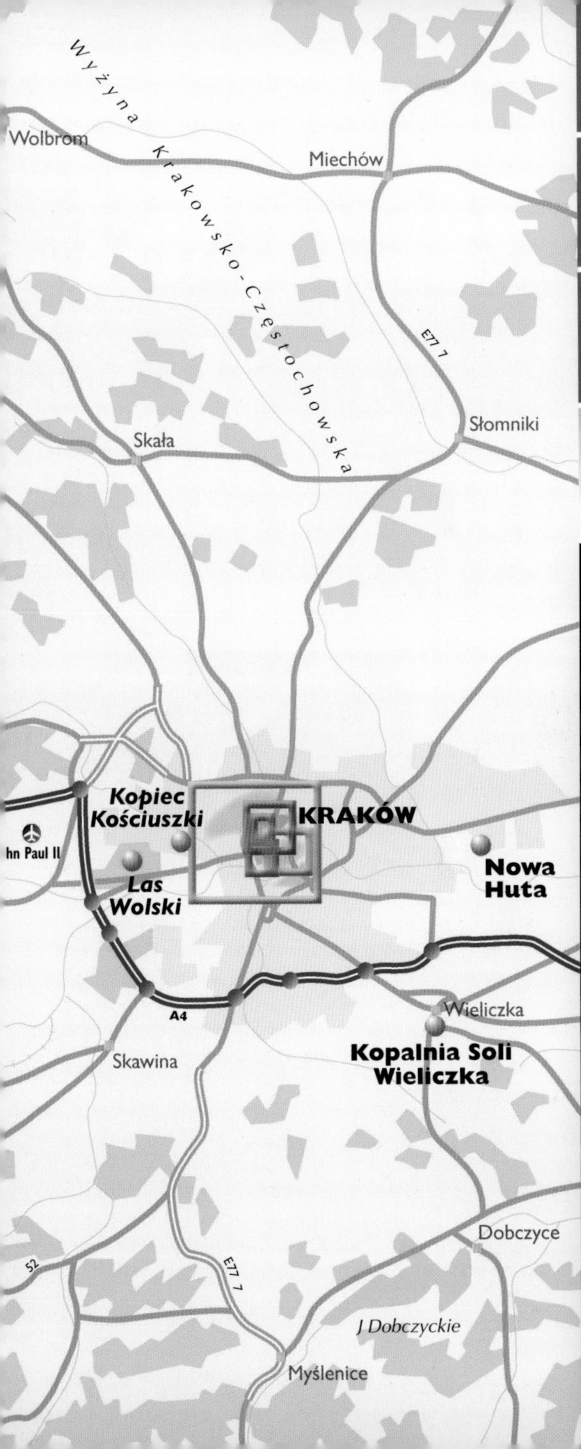

Kopiec Kościuszki

KRAKÓW

hn Paul II

Las Wolski

Nowa Huta

A4

Wieliczka

Skawina

Kopalnia Soli Wieliczka

52

E77

Dobczyce

J Dobczyckie

Myślenice

Auschwitz-Birkenau

TOP 25

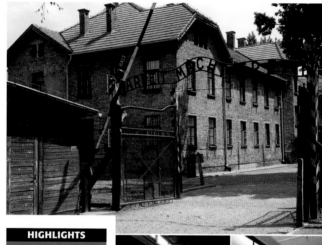

- Gate with the motto "Arbeit Macht Frei"
- Film of the camp's liberation
- Heaps of prisoners' effects: shoes, spectacles, suitcases
- Mounds of hair shorn from prisoners
- Birkenau barracks, unloading ramp, railway
- Ruins of gas chambers and crematoria
- Moving photographs

TIPS

- You cannot know whether the person next to you lost a relative or even their whole family in the camp. It's important to be respectful—particularly of the "no photographs" rule.
- Visits are not recommended for under-14s.

Many visitors to Krakow feel they must see the Nazi concentration camp, but consider whether it's the right time for you to go. It's a powerfully emotional experience and maybe not something to slot casually into a city break.

Extermination camp The Nazis brought the first slave laborers, mainly Polish political prisoners, to Auschwitz in 1940. Many soon died because of the appalling conditions working for the German industries that relocated here; others starved to death, were executed or died from torture or medical experiments. In 1941, Soviet prisoners of war were brought to the extermination camp at nearby Birkenau. By 1942, the camp was receiving Jews from all over Europe and became one of the main sites

Clockwise from far left: The entrance to Auschwitz, with "Arbeit Macht Frei" ("Work Sets You Free") above the gates; the main SS guardhouse at Birkenau, known as the Death Gate; part of the Extermination exhibition; Material Evidence of the Crime exhibition; sleeping quarters in the quarantine block at Birkenau

THE BASICS

www.auschwitz.org

✚ See map ▷ 98

✉ ul. Więźniów Oświęcimia 20, Oświęcim

☎ 33 844 8099 (Mon–Fri 7–3)

🕓 Site of the camp Dec–Feb daily 8–3; Mar, Nov 8–4; Apr, Oct 8–5; May, Sep 8–6; Jun–Aug 8–7. Whole site closed 1 Jan, Easter Sunday, 25 Dec and for special events (posted on website)

🍴 Cafeteria (€)

🚌 Oświęcim train station, then one of several local buses to the Auschwitz site. Shuttle bus runs between Auschwitz and Birkenau (3km/2 miles) 15 Apr–31 Oct

🚏 Oświęcim

♿ Few; flat site but not all the museum is accessible

🎧 Museum free; headphones, film, inexpensive; English-language guided group tours of 3 hours 30 min moderate (book ahead); longer study tours

of the Nazi drive to wipe out the Jewish race. Unloaded after days traveling in cattle trucks, those judged unfit to work were ordered into "shower rooms"—gas chambers that killed up to 2,000 at a time. It is estimated that between 1 and 1.5 million people died here before the camp was liberated in 1945.

Lessons of history Auschwitz is now a living memorial to those who died here and to the horror of the Final Solution. The museum at Auschwitz has piles of personal possessions taken from the prisoners. In the barracks at Birkenau the wooden bunks would collapse under the weight of the many prisoners crowded into each one. You'll also find the remnants of the gas chambers and crematoria. The ashes of the dead still lie in the ground here.

Kopalnia Soli Wieliczka

HIGHLIGHTS

● St. Kinga's Chapel
● Warsaw Chamber
● Pieskowa Skała Chamber
● Erazm Barącz Chamber
● Weimar Chamber
● 36m-high (118ft) Stanisław Staszic Chamber

DID YOU KNOW?

● Many famous people have visited the salt mines, from the poet Goethe onward. Recent celebrities include George Bush Senior, Britain's Prince Edward and Ritchie Blackmore of the band Deep Purple.

● The underground microclimate is helpful for people with respiratory problems and the mine runs its own treatment center (see website for details).

TIP

● Visitors have to wait until there is a group of 35 for a tour in their own language. In practice, this wait is never longer than an hour and often shorter. At quiet times of year, call or check the website for times of English-language tours.

A visit to a salt mine sounds grim, doesn't it? But this is a great half-day out from Krakow. The jaws of more than a million people a year drop when they see the vast underground chambers.

Grey gold There have been saltworks at Wieliczka from neolithic times, but mining and the sale of the valuable rock salt began in earnest in the 11th century, with the oldest known shaft in the mine dating back to the 13th century. The wealth it brought to Krakow belonged to its rulers. In medieval times it made up about a third of royal revenue and paid for much of the rich architecture you see in the city today. Commercial mining has now stopped and the mine is purely a popular tourist attraction.

Clockwise from far left: The Great Chamber; the top of the Daniłowicz shaft; salt sculptures carved by the miners; St. Kinga's Chapel; religious carvings in salt; a guide at the salt mine; the entrance above ground

THE BASICS

www.wieliczka-saltmine.com

See map ▷ 99

ul. Daniłowicza 10, Wieliczka

12 278 7302, 12 278 7366

Apr–Oct daily 7.30–7.30; Nov–Mar 8–5; Easter Sun 7.30–2.30.

Cafeteria above ground; simple restaurant at end of tour below ground (€)

Wieliczka Kopalnia, bus 304 from the main bus station

Wieliczka Rynek, from Krakow main station

Excellent: $1m-worth of elevators, ramps and toilets make the most popular sections wheelchair-accessible

Expensive; fee for taking pictures inexpensive

Going deep The hardest part of the two-and-a-half-hour tour is the first descent, a walk down 378 steps. After that it's an easy, spacious, well-lit route, covering about 2km (1 mile). The deepest you go is 135m (443ft) below ground level. The mine is much more extensive than this, however: it goes down to 327m (1,073ft) with nearly 3,000 chambers on nine levels. The Daniłowicz shaft used by visitors was first sunk in 1635 and reaches down to 243m (797ft). As well as seeing the wooden mine workings, you will see carvings and sculptures made by the miners in the salt, underground lakes and huge ornate chambers used for all sorts of events from weddings to orchestral concerts. A lift brings you back to the surface at the end of the tour.

More to See

KOPIEC KOŚCIUSZKI

About 3.5km (2 miles) from the center of the city, this monument to Tadeusz Kościuszko, dating from the 1820s and restored in the 2000s, is a pleasant walk out of town on a fine day, with good views of the city along the way. There is also a small museum to the hero in the old fortifications.

➕ B5 ✉ al. Waszyngtona 1 ☎ 12 425 1116 🕐 Daily 9–dusk; also evening opening with separate ticket May–Sep daily dusk–11pm; museum daily 9.30–4.30 🍴 Café with outside terrace (€) 🚋 Tram 1, 2, 6 to Salwator then bus 100 from Salwator, or 101 from Rondo Grunwaldzkie ♿ Circular path to the top of the mount is steep 🚹 Inexpensive; separate ticket for small waxwork museum inexpensive

LAS WOLSKI

Home to Krakow's zoo (▷ 106) and Piłsudski's Mound, this forest west of the city between ul. Królowej Jadwigi and the Vistula has eight walking routes, a winter ski route and a bike route, as well

as several examples of traditional wooden architecture.

➕ See map ▷ 99 🚌 102, 134, 152

NOWA HUTA

www.mhk.pl

If you are interested in seeing the Soviet Union's influence on Poland, visit this suburb, built on Stalin's orders in the 1940s. It's very spread out so allow a lot of time, or take a tour from Krakow. The Sendzimir steelworks are now owned by an Indian global industrialist, but "Our Lord's Ark," the Queen of Poland Church, built in 1977, is a dramatic symbol of Polish resistance to the Soviet way of doing things. Visit the local museum first to get your bearings.

➕ See map ▷ 99 ✉ Museum of the History of Nowa Huta, os. Słoneczne 16 ☎ 12 425 9775 🕐 Apr–Oct Tue–Sun and second Sun of month 9.30–5; Nov–Mar Tue, Thu–Sat 9–4, Wed 10–5, second Sun of month 9–4. Closed Tue after second Sun 🚋 Tram 4 to plac Centralny 🚹 Museum inexpensive, Wed free

Cycling in Las Wolski

The crucifixion in the Queen of Poland Church, Nowa Huta

Excursions

CZĘSTOCHOWA

Home of Poland's holiest shrine, Częstochowa's Jana Góra monastery is not only of interest to pilgrims but to anyone who wants to explore its people's passionate relationship with the Catholic religion and how it is entwined in the country's history.

Jasna Góra has at its heart the icon of the Black Madonna, already several centuries old when Pauline monks first came to the "bright hill" in 1382. The scars on the Virgin's face date from a 15th-century robbery attempt. The Gothic chapel was begun shortly after, while numerous attacks led to the fortification of the hill. In 1655, a tiny number of troops and monks held off a seige by 3,000 Swedes—a miracle that inspired the rest of the conquered country to rise up and repel the invaders. The icon became a symbol of a free Poland.

THE BASICS

Distance: 140km (87 miles)
Journey time: 2–3 hours by coach from Dworzec bus station; 90 mins–2 hours by train from Dworzec Główny
🛈 al. Najświętszej Maryi Panny 65 ☎ 34 368 2250; www.cestochowa.pl
🕒 Mon–Sat 9–5
Jasna Góra
www.jasnagora.pl
✉ ul. O. A. Kordeckiego 2
☎ 34 377 7777
💲 Expensive
❓ You need to pre-book a tour to see the icon

ZAKOPANE

A winter sports and summer hiking center high in the jagged Tatra Mountains, Poland's winter capital is also popular with visitors who just want to breathe the mountain air and sample the traditional highlander, or *góralski,* way of life.

The easiest mountain resort to reach from Krakow, and a ski resort for more than 100 years, Zakopane has also been an attraction for Poland's great artists, including the writer and painter Witkiewicz, who in the 1890s, by designing Willa (Villa) Koliba, instigated the "Zakopane style" of ornamental wooden buildings, much copied today. The legacy is a town that has more than a century of cultural heritage, as well as 50 ski lifts and 160km (100 miles) of ski runs. Hikers will take the mountain stream rushing along the main street as their starting point for exploring some of the 240km (149 miles) of marked trails in the Tatra National Park.

THE BASICS

Distance: 100km (62 miles)
Journey time: 2 hours or more by bus from Dworzec bus station depending on traffic; 2.5–3.5 hours by train from Dworzec Główny
Willa Koliba
✉ ul. Kościelska 18
☎ 18 201 3602; www. muzeumtatrzanskie.pl
🕒 Wed–Sat 9–5, Sun 9–3
♿ None 💲 Inexpensive
Tatrzański Park Narodowy (Tatra National Park Office)
www.tpn.pl
✉ ul. Kuźnice 1 ☎ 18 202 3300

Entertainment and Nightlife

AQUA PARK

www.parkwodny.pl

The biggest indoor aqua park in Poland, to the northeast of Krakow center, is the place to take the children when they need to splash about. Attractions include pipes and slides, tthe Rapid River and a saline sauna as well as lane swimming, and climbing walls for dry fun.

✚ Off map ✉ ul. Dobrego Pasterza 126 ☎ 12 616 3190 ⏰ Daily 8am–10pm 🍴 Restaurant (€) 🚌 128 ♿ Good 💷 Moderate

GOLF

www.krakow-valley.com

This 18-hole championship golf course to the northwest of the city offers a driving range, shooting range, horse riding and skiing in winter.

✚ Off map ✉ 328 Miejscowość Paczółtowice, 32-063 Krzeszowice ☎ 12 258 6000 ⏰ Daily 🚌 From Krakow main stations to Paczółtowice 💷 Expensive

KRAKOW ZOO

www.zoo-krakow.pl

Set in the middle of Las Wolski, the 17ha (42-acre) zoo has several successful breeding programs and has raised litters of snow leopards, Chinese leopards, jaguars and pythons. Other rare animals include a herd of endangered pygmy hippopotamuses and Przewalski horses, which are extinct in the wild. There's also a petting zoo.

✚ Off map ✉ ul. Kasy Oszczędności Miasta Krakowa 14 ☎ 12 425 3551, 12 425 3552 ⏰ Summer daily 9–7; spring and fall 9–5; winter 9–3 🚌 134 from Cracovia Hotel ♿ Few 💷 Moderate

Restaurants

PRICES

Prices are approximate, based on a 3-course meal for one person.
€€€ over 170PLN/€50
€€ 100–170PLN/ €30–€50
€ under 100PLN/€30

CHATA ZBÓJNICKA (€)

www.chatazbojnicka. zakopane.biz

The name means "robber's hut" and this rustic hideaway is set back from the road. The log fire in winter, garden in summer and the *góralski* (mountain) cooking extend a warm welcome.

✚ Off map ✉ ul. Jagiellońska, Zakopane ☎ 18 201 4217 ⏰ Daily 5pm–midnight

KARCZMA CZARCI JAR (€)

www.czarcijar.pl

Expect Polish and traditional *góralski* dishes at this rustic pine cabin. You'll be serenaded by a highland band.

✚ Off map ✉ ul. Małe Żywczańskie 11a, Zakopane ☎ 18 206 4178 ⏰ Daily 1–11

KARCZMA OBROCHTÓWKA (€)

www.obrochtowka-zakopane.pl

Enjoy well-prepared traditional highland dishes in a traditional Zakopane inn. There is a summer garden and an evening folk band.

✚ Off map ✉ ul. Kraszewskiego 10a, Zakopane ☎ 18 206 2979 ⏰ Daily 12–10

KARCZMA SABALA (€€)

www.sabala.zakopane.pl

Named after a famous folksinger and in a century-old hotel on Zakopane's main street, Sabala has a terrace and old wooden ceilings. The menu features highland and international dishes.

✚ Off map ✉ ul. Krupówki 11, Zakopane ☎ 18 201 5092 ⏰ Daily 11am–midnight

With a tradition of welcoming guests that stretches back centuries, Krakow knows about hospitality. Some of the grand old hotels have been renovated, but you'll also find a choice of good budget hotels.

Introduction

Since the city is popular year-round, try to book your hotel as much in advance as possible. You'll discover a wide variety of accommodations, from smart modern chain hotels to hostels and simple, sparsely furnished apartments, with a range of good-value places in between.

Sleep with history

For the first-time visitor it makes sense to try to stay in or near the Old Town so that all the sights are within easy reach. As an alternative, visitors interested in Jewish history might want to consider Kazimierz, where new hotels, guest houses and tourist apartments are opening all the time, although the district cannot match the Old Town's luxurious renovated palaces or the facilities of the large, purpose-built hotels that ring the Planty. The young and fashionable also like Kazimierz because of its indie bars and clubs and cutting-edge atmosphere, even if it is still crumbling around the edges a little bit.

Local streets

Even beyond the Planty, you may still be within an easy walk of the center and its sights. What you lose by not having a museum as a neighbor you might gain from quieter nights by not having a hip cellar bar disgorging rowdy revelers into your street in the early hours. Public transportation is good and easy to negotiate and taxis are inexpensive, so if you do find yourself outside the central districts— perhaps staying in student accommodations on the city outskirts in summer—do not despair. Cinderella will still be able to get back from the nightclub, by nightbus if need be.

PRICES

Note that even hotels that quote prices in euros will expect to be paid in zloty at the current rate of exchange. If you stay longer than one night, your bill will include a small tourist tax.

Top to bottom: Hotel Eden; a hotel restaurant; bath treats at Hotel Copernicus; the rooftop terrace at Hotel Stary

Budget Hotels

PRICES

Expect to pay up to 250PLN (€75) a night for a double room in a budget hotel.

CRACOW B&B

www.cracowbb.com

Crisp, modern and spotlessly clean, this B&B near the main railway station is a great budget choice, with its parquet floors, trendy furnishings and breakfast in bed. Rooms are huge and there's a kitchen for guest use with free tea and coffee. The only downside is the shared bathroom.

🚇 M2 ✉ ul. Moniuszki 24 ☎ 604 903 733 🚋 Tram to Rondo Mogilska

CYBULSKIEGO GUEST ROOMS

www.freerooms.pl

Arranged in apartments with private shower rooms and kitchen facilities, the 14 plainly furnished beds here would suit anyone on a budget who needs more privacy than hostels provide. You get your own front door key, helpful staff, excellent WiFi, and good buffet breakfast.

🚇 G3 ✉ ul. Cybulskiego 6 ☎ 12 423 0532

HOTEL CHOPIN

www.vi-hotels.com

Large, three-star chain hotel just outside the historical center featuring standard rooms fitted out with everything the traveler needs on the road.

🚇 M3 ✉ Przy Rondzie 2 ☎ 12 299 0000 🚋 Tram to Rondo Mogilska

HOTEL GRAND FELIX

www.hotelgrandfelix.pl

For a different take on Krakow, stay at this 50-room business hotel in Nowa Huta. Sleep, surf the web, shower and breakfast in a bland but well-kept environment—then catch a tram to the city center.

🚇 Off map ✉ os. Złotej Jesieni 12 ☎ 12 681 8600 🚋 Tram to Rondo Hipokratesa

IBIS KRAKOW CENTRUM

www.ibishotel.com

Close to the Vistula and Wawel, though without views, and 10 minutes' walk from the Old Town, this is an efficiently run chain hotel with 175 rooms. Good for late and early breakfasts and dinners. There's a summer beer garden.

🚇 G5 ✉ ul. Syrokomli 2 ☎ 12 299 3300 🚋 Tram 2 to Jubilat ♿ 6 adapted rooms

KRAKOW'S HOSTELS

In addition to hotels of all categories, Krakow has around 60 hostels. These often have funky themes, such as Tutti Frutti with its fruit posters and B-Movie with its movie theme. Prices for a dorm bed start at a mere 30PLN a night.

KLEZMER HOIS

www.klezmer.pl

Budget travelers will be interested in the four rooms on the second floor of this 10-room hotel near the Remuh Synagogue. They have been neatly renovated, with the odd antique giving things an olde-worlde feel, though only two have their own bathroom. The restaurant downstairs (▷ 84) is one of Kazimierz's best Jewish eateries.

🚇 K5 ✉ ul. Szeroka 6 ☎ 12 411 1245 🚋 Tram 2 to Rakowicka

MARIE CURIE

Only bookable through popular booking websites, this rambling guest house has modern, well-maintained rooms but no reception (you need a code to enter, which is emailed to you). The big plus is the location near the Old Town and the main station.

🚇 J3 ✉ ul. Marie Curie Skłodowskiej 🚋 Tram to Dworzec Główny

PIANO GUEST HOUSE

www.pianoguesthouse.com

Inexpensive guest house near the main station, with friendly owners, stylish breakfast room and basic but clean and comfortable rooms. Breakfast included and tours available.

🚇 K1 ✉ ul. Kątowa ☎ 12 632 1371 🚋 Tram 2 to Rakowicka

Mid-Range Hotels

PRICES

Expect to pay between 250PLN (€75) and 500PLN (€150) a night for a double room in a mid-range hotel.

ART HOTEL NIEBIESKI
www.niebieski.com.pl
Half the 13 rooms in this elegant old building near the Salwator monastery have views over the Vistula and Wawel Hill. Bathrooms have heated floors and showers and it's all decorated in modern Polish romantic style. There's a spa to unwind in, and underground parking.
➕ F6 ✉ ul. Flisacka 3
☎ 12 297 4000 🚊 Tram 1, 2, 6 to Salwator

FRANCUSKI HOTEL
www.hotel-francuski.com
Madly modern when it first opened in 1912, this 42-room honeymooners' favorite near St. Florian's Gate has a grand fin-de-siècle feel though the facilities, including wellness center and WiFi, are up to date. Parking, children and even pets welcome.
➕ J3 ✉ ul. Pijarska 13
☎ 666 195 831

HOTEL AMADEUS
www.hotel-amadeus.pl
Tucked away near the Mały Rynek, this 14th-century town house with a 17th-century St. Mary of the Rosary painted on its facade has been favored by princes, ambassadors and the dancer Mikhail Barishnikov. The 22 traditionally styled rooms have modern facilities including Jacuzzi baths. There is a fitness room, sauna and guarded car parking.
➕ J4 ✉ ul. Mikołajska 20
☎ 12 429 6070

HOTEL EDEN
www.hoteleden.pl
On the Kazimierz site where, legend has it, the founder of the Izaak Synagogue discovered treasure in his garden, this hotel has deep Jewish roots. The 27 characterless rooms have all modern facilities, and there is also a sauna, salt grotto and ritual Mikvah bath (open to nonguests and said to be the only one in Poland) on site. The restaurant serves kosher food.
➕ K6 ✉ ul. Ciemna 15
☎ 12 430 6565

WIRED OR NOT

Nearly all Krakow's hotels and hostels now have internet and WiFi, but not always in all rooms. The best internet access is in luxury hotels and, conversely, hostels, which often offer a computer terminal or two for you to check your emails. It's in the mid-range that internet facilities can be patchy. Check when booking.

HOTEL ESTER
www.hotel-ester.krakow.pl
Right in the center of Kazimierz, overlooking the Remuh, Popper and Old synagogues, this traditional hotel with 32 rooms has an elevator and a restaurant with live *klezmer* music on weekends.
➕ K5 ✉ ul. Szeroka 20
☎ 12 429 1188

HOTEL KARMEL
www.karmel.com.pl
In Kazimierz, between ul. Szeroka and Plac Nowy, the Karmel has 11 traditionally styled bedrooms in a 19th-century building with an Italian restaurant in its aged cellar.
➕ K6 ✉ ul. Kupa 15 ☎ 12 430 6697 🚊 Tram 3, 9, 24 to ul. Miodowa

HOTEL POLLERA
www.pollera.com.pl
Just across the Planty from the main station, this very well appointed and characterful hotel has a history going back to 1834. The elegant rooms are done out with antique-style furniture, and all have their own modern-ish bathrooms. The high-ceilinged restaurant is used only for breakfast, or you can ask for croissants and coffee in your room.
➕ J3 ✉ ul. Szpitalna 30
☎ 12 422 1044

HOTEL SASKI
www.hotelsaski.com.pl
A few steps off the Rynek Główny, this grande dame

of Krakow's hotel scene is the place to head for a bit of central European style without the crippling bill at check-out. While the styling of the building is all art nouveau, rooms are fairly standard and some don't have their own bathrooms.

➕ H3 ✉ ul. Sławkowska 3 ☎ 12 421 4222

HOTEL SENACKI

www.hotelsenacki.pl

Opposite the church of Św. Piotra i Pawła and a 24-hour supermarket on the Royal Route to Wawel, this 20-room hotel in a 14th-century house is traditionally decorated. There is a café-bar in the 13th-century cellar and a ground-floor restaurant with a venerable beamed ceiling and carved stone pillars. The staff are knowledgeable and very helpful.

➕ H4 ✉ ul. Grodzka 51 ☎ 12 422 7686

NOVOTEL

www.novotel.com

With 198 rooms and right on the river but still an easy walk from the Old Town, this contemporary hotel is well designed, with a separate executive floor as well as a children's play corner within easy sight of the lobby-bar. Many bedrooms have a Wawel view. Other facilities include a garden brasserie, pool, Jacuzzi, sauna, gym and spa center.

➕ G5 ✉ ul. Tadeusza Kościuszki 5 ☎ 12 299 2900

NOVOTEL KRAKOW CITY WEST

www.novotel.com

Outside town in a nothing suburb near blocks of student accommodations, this friendly, efficiently run hotel with 304 rooms was built in 1976 as the first Holiday Inn behind the Iron Curtain. Recently upgraded facilities include an indoor pool, sauna and casino. There are also a bar and a restaurant with children's menu. Good for families.

➕ C2 ✉ al. Armii Krajowej 11 ☎ 12 622 6400 🚌 208 and free hotel shuttle buses into the city center

POD WAWELEM

www.hotelpodwawelem.pl

A cool place to stay, with a warm welcome, in a stunning location for the price, between the Sheraton and Wawel Hill on the banks of the Vistula. There are 48 contemporary-style rooms

ROOM WRINKLES

It seems to be a near-universal practice for hotels in Krakow to charge a rate for the room regardless of how many people are staying in it. Do check, however, as there are exceptions. Also be aware that some hotels' rates include breakfast and others do not.

sandwiched between a roof-top café-bar with exceptional views and a cellar bar. It also has fitness and steam rooms.

➕ G5 ✉ plac Na Groblach 22 ☎ 12 426 2625

PURO

www.purohotel.pl

This funkily sophisticated glass cube near the main station and Krakowska mall has trendy, retro-styled public spaces but 21st-century rooms. Bathrooms are of the latest design, the room color schemes are cool but relaxing and there are useful extras like free WiFi in your room, free international phone calls and underground parking.

➕ J2 ✉ ul. Ogrodowa 10 ☎ 12 314 2100

RADISSON BLU KRAKOW

www.radissonblu.com

In a new, elegant building next to the Philharmonic Hall on the edge of the Planty, the 196 rooms, though geared to business travelers, offer reliable quality for a city break. Amenities include air-conditioning, underground parking, 24-hour room service, gym and sauna. On-site eating options include Solfez international-style restaurant, Milk&Co for Małopolska dishes, and the Salt&Co café-bar with salt walls.

➕ H4 ✉ ul. Straszewskiego 17 ☎ 12 618 8888

Luxury Hotels

HOTEL COPERNICUS

www.hotel.com.pl

In Krakow's most historic street under Wawel Hill, behind a 14th-century facade, this hotel has all the modern features you might want, including a small pool in the Gothic cellars, a roof terrace air-conditioning, and the decor and relaxed feel of a boutique hotel. The 29 rooms have friezes fit for a Renaissance prince, beamed ceilings and restored fragments of medieval wall painting.

➕ H5 ✉ ul. Kanonicza 16
☎ 12 424 3400

HOTEL GRÓDEK

www.donimirski.com

A sympathetically restored former palace with 23 rooms in a quiet spot next to a Dominican convent, the Gródek is a short walk from the main market square. Each room is individually decorated, but all have air-conditioning and up-to-date bathrooms paired with antique-style furniture. The hotel has its own archaeological museum of finds made during the conversion of the 16th-century building.

➕ J4 ✉ ul. Na Gródku 4
☎ 12 431 9030

HOTEL MALTAŃSKI

www.donimirski.com

This is a true boutique hotel in green surroundings on the edge of the Planty near the Franciscan church in the Old Town. In a complex of three low, white buildings full of character and as rich in history as any in Krakow (the names Lubomirski, Czartoryski and Potocki feature), the 16 pretty rooms don't disappoint. Good facilities include business services and guarded parking.

➕ H5 ✉ ul. Straszewskiego 4 ☎ 12 431 0010

HOTEL STARY

www.stary.hotel.com.pl

Named for the Stary Theater nearby, this hotel has been chicly converted from an ancient building in the Old Town. Some of the 53 rooms are contemporary, others more historical with original frescoes. The

vaulted cellars house two pools, a fitness center, and a health-giving salt cave. There is a rooftop restaurant and a café-bar with views of the Mariacki church.

➕ H3 ✉ ul. Szczepańska 5
☎ 12 384 0808

OSTOYA PALACE HOTEL

www.ostoyapalace.pl

In a romantic 19th-century building just outside the Planty, the 24 rooms have old doors, parquet floors and traditional tiled stoves, but also air-conditioning and showers rather than baths, though one suite has a whirlpool bath. There's an on-site restaurant too.

➕ G4 ✉ ul. Piłsudskiego 24
☎ 12 430 9000

POD RÓŻĄ

www.hotel.com.pl

The oldest hotel in the city goes back to the 17th century. Its motto is "Let this house last as long as an ant does not drink all the water from the seas and a tortoise walk around the whole world." Franz Liszt and Tsar Alexander I both stayed here, "Under the Sign of the Rose," on the Royal Route. The 57 rooms have marble bathrooms and heated floors, yet original frescoes remain. There's also a gym with rooftop views.

➕ J3 ✉ ul. Floriańska 14
☎ 12 424 3300

Krakow is a relaxed, well-organized, fun city. Once you've arrived from the airport you will be able to walk almost everywhere you want to go, but if you do use public transport, you'll find it is safe, clean and punctual, and the locals are helpful.

Planning Ahead

WHEN TO GO

Krakow has a temperate climate with frequent changes in the weather. Carry an umbrella and something warm. May and June tend to be best—the weather is good and the city buzzes with festivals. Summer is busy; winter days are cold but the Christmas market is in town.

TIME

L Krakow is on Central European Time, 1 hour ahead of London, 6 hours ahead of New York.

AVERAGE DAILY MAXIMUM TEMPERATURES

JAN	FEB	MAR	APR	MAY	JUN	JUL	AUG	SEP	OCT	NOV	DEC
33°F	37°F	46°F	56°F	67°F	71°F	74°F	74°F	65°F	56°F	43°F	36°F
1°C	3°C	8°C	13°C	19°C	22°C	23°C	23°C	18°C	13°C	6°C	2°C

Spring (Mar–Apr) Very variable, with showers and sun by turns.
Summer (May–August) Hot but western winds bring storms and rain.
Autumn (Sep–Oct) Variable but can be dry, sunny and crisp with golden days.
Winter (Nov–Feb) Eastern winds mean less rain, but the cold can be penetrating and it can snow, particularly in January.

WHAT'S ON

January Carnival season.
February Processions of hooded Brothers of the Good Death at Franciscan church every Fri in Lent. *International Sea Shanty Festival.*
March *Misteria Paschalia* music festival. Holy Week and Good Friday services. *Bach Days* music festival.
April All Fools' Day. Easter. *Easter Beethoven* music festival.
May Polish Flag Day. Constitution Day. *Cracovia Marathon.* St. Stanisław procession: Wawel to Skałka. *Corpus Christi*: procession with scattering of flower petals. *Cracow Screen Festival.*

Juwenalia student festival. *Night of Museums:* special events. *Lajkonik parade* (Thu after Corpus Christi). *Film Music Festival.* Photography month: exhibitions citywide.
June *Krakow Festival. Children's Day. Open Gardens Festival.* Pageant to enthrone the cockerel king of the Brotherhood of Riflemen. *Wianki* festival: floating wreaths with candles on the Vistula, all-night merrymaking, music and fireworks. *Grand Dragon Parade.*
July Festivals of Jewish culture, military bands, jazz, Carpathian music.
August Folk festival. *Pierogi* food festival.

September *Sacrum Profanum* festival of contemporary music.
October Month of *Encounters with Jewish Culture, Organ Music Days, Krakow Book Fair.*
November All Saints' Day and All Souls' Day: flowers and candles put on graves. Independence Day. Krakow's Christmas market opens on Rynek Główny. *Zaduszki* jazz festival
December *Feast of Mikolaj:* St. Nicholas brings children gifts. Christmas cribs on show (morning of first Thursday in December) in Rynek Główny. *Sylwester:* New Year's Eve celebrations.

KRAKOW ONLINE
www.krakow.pl
The city government site is an invaluable source of information. It includes an official accommodations booking system and comprehensive listings for theaters, cinemas, galleries and other cultural centers.

www.biurofestiwalowe.pl
Krakow's Festival Office coordinates the plethora of events and festivals in the city. Useful for looking up dates of the many movable feasts.

www.mhk.pl
The website of the Historical Museum of the City of Krakow should be your first stop for information about Krakow's main attractions. It not only details what's on in all its many branches but also helps you decode the sometimes byzantine opening times.

www.mnk.pl
The official website of the National Museum covers the many museums run by the state, not the city—most of which concentrate on art or a particular artist, such as the Czartoryski Museum and the Mehoffer House. The English version of the website is under construction.

www.karnet.krakow.pl
The official listings guide is more useful to you if your interests turn toward art and Chopin rather than Irish pubs and death metal.

www.krakow-info.com
This is similar to the other listings sites, but worth looking at for its handy hints pages and tips for visitors with disabilities.

TRAVEL SITES

www.poland.travel
Official site of the Polish National Tourist Office, useful for background information and planning trips farther afield.
www.mcit.pl
Tourist Information service for Małopolska, the region around Krakow, which organizes tours from its office at ul. Grodzka 31.
www.zakopane-life.com
Listings and information helpful for anyone traveling south to the mountains.
www.fodors.com
A complete travel-planning site. You can research prices and weather; book air tickets, cars and rooms; ask questions (and get answers) from fellow travelers.

INTERNET ACCESS

As in most Western cities it is easy to access the internet in Krakow via your phone or laptop. Every café, hotel and restaurant has WiFi, as do the Rynek Głowny and the center of Kazimierz.

NEED TO KNOW PLANNING AHEAD

Getting There

VISAS AND INSURANCE

Poland is within the 26-state Schengen Agreement area and no visa is required for citizens of other Schengen countries. There's no limit to how long other EU nationals can stay, but passport holders from the US, Canada, Australia and New Zealand will need a visa for a visit longer than 90 days. In certain circumstances visitors from those countries who do not hold full passports will need a visa; visitors from other countries may also need one. Check before traveling on the Polish Ministry of Foreign Affairs website at www.msz.gov.pl. Medical care is good in Krakow but you will need adequate travel insurance. Although EU citizens can use an EHIC card, it is not wise to rely solely on this.

TIPS

● If traveling to or from Krakow by train, check out the excellent www.seat61. com website, which has lots of tips.
● Luggage with wheels is handy in Krakow. It is easy to get from the train or the bus station into the center of the Old Town using the wide, ramped underpass.

AIRPORTS

There are direct flights to Krakow from Europe and North America into Krakow's John Paul II International Airport (also known as Krakow-Balice) which also receives many charter flights.

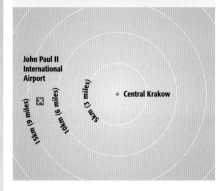

John Paul II International Airport

15km (9 miles) 10km (6 miles) 5km (3 miles)

● Central Krakow

FROM THE AIRPORT

All flights arrive at Krakow's John Paul II International Airport (1 ul. kpt. Medweckiego, Balice, tel 0801 055 000, www.krakowairport. pl), about 12km (8 miles) from the city center. In the international terminal you will find tourist information, facilities for visitors with disabilities, mother and baby rooms, foreign exchange facilities and cashpoint machines, a bank (Mon–Fri 8–8, Sat–Sun 9.15–8), a post office (Mon–Fri 8–2.45), shops and cafés and lost luggage (tel 12 285 5121). You'll also find desks for all the main car-rental companies and a 24-hour car park (tel 12 639 3065 or 12 295 3178; the cost is 9PLN an hour, 49PLN a day).

Taxis are metered and will give you a receipt *(paragon)* if requested. Depending on traffic, it's a 20- to 30-minute drive to the Old Town and will cost 60–70PLN. To call the airport's official taxi company, dial 12 258 0258. Your hotel or hostel may well offer to send a car to meet you and this may be slightly cheaper.

Buses 208 and 292 leave from a stop just past the train shuttle bus stop—turn right on leaving the international terminal. Not very

frequent (departures are about 40 minutes apart), they stop everywhere on the way into the city and take the better part of an hour to get to the main station. A ticket machine at the stop takes coins and has ticket information in English. A kiosk upstairs in the international terminal also sells bus tickets or you can pay the driver. One-way tickets are 4PLN.

Otherwise, take a shuttle bus from just outside the international arrivals hall to catch the fast and efficient train from the airport to the city's main station (Dworzec Główny). The whole journey will probably take nearer to half an hour than the advertised 15 minutes and trains leave approximately every half-hour. You can buy tickets (8PLN) on the train or before boarding.

BY BUS

The main bus terminal is next to the main train station and has an entrance from ul. Bosacka. There's a helpful English-language version of its website, www.rda.krakow.pl, with departure times and a ticket sales portal. The international ticket office at the terminal is open daily 7am–7.45pm (tel 12 393 5255). Eurolines runs international buses to Krakow from many European cities. For details of routes, tickets and 15- and 30-day European passes see its website (www.eurolines.com). Its partner company in Poland is Arriva Eurolines Polska (tel 703 303 333, www.arrivabus.pl).

BY RAIL

Trains from the airport, from other parts of Poland and the rest of Europe arrive and depart from the main station, Dworzec Główny, just outside the Planty and the Old Town. There are left-luggage facilities. The express to Warsaw takes about two and a half hours. Useful websites for rail travel within Poland are www.rozklad-pkp.pl and www.intercity.pl. For expresses and trains into and out of Poland, see www.polrail.com. There are direct trains to Krakow from Prague, Budapest, Vienna and Berlin.

DEPARTURES

● On leaving Krakow by train for the airport, be aware that if you buy a ticket in advance it will be timed and will be valid only for two hours after the time for which it is issued. It's also quite a long walk from the station entrance and the ticket office to the departure platform for the airport train, so leave yourself lots of time.

● Security at Krakow-Balice airport is very strict. You will not be allowed to take any container larger than 100ml through security in your hand luggage. This covers everything from full bottles of vodka to empty crystal vases. You'll need a permit to export anything made before 1945 (details on www.poland.travel).

DRIVING

It's only worth driving to Krakow if your visit to the city is part of a longer road journey in Europe. The main international motorways serving Krakow are the A4 (from Germany through Wrocław, Katowice, Krakow, Tarnów and Rzeszów into the Ukraine) and the A7 from Gdańsk through Warsaw and Krakow to Slovakia.

Getting Around

ON TWO FEET

The best way to see Krakow is to walk. It's a compact, mainly flat city and on a short visit you'll scarcely need to use public transport if you are staying in the Old Town or Kazimierz. Many companies run walking tours, which are a good way of orienting yourself. There is a huge variety in Krakow, catering for all tastes. Krakow Daily Walks is one of the most popular (meet in front of the Tourist Information Office, at Plac Mariacki 3, tel 12 430 2117, www. krakow-travel.com, costing 50PLN) for the Old Town walk.

BUSES AND TRAMS

The city-run buses and trams operate a good service including night buses in and around Krakow (see www.mpk.krakow.pl). Buy tickets from machines at bus and tram stops (these usually give change but don't take notes), nearby kiosks and machines on some of the newer buses. The ticket machines have information in English too. If you buy a ticket on board from the driver you will have to pay a supplement of 0.50PLN. There are also higher rates for buses operating within the larger metropolitan area.

Buses and trams operate a flat-fare system within the city boundaries:

- 3.80PLN for single ticket
- 5PLN for a 60-minute ticket (useful for journeys involving two buses or a bus and a tram, such as from the center to Kopiec Kościuszko)
- 15PLN for a 24-hour ticket (good if you are planning on taking a night bus or two)
- 24PLN for a 48-hour ticket
- 36PLN for a 72-hour ticket
- 48PLN for a weekly ticket.

Reduced-price tickets are available for children, senior citizens and family (for example a family weekend ticket costs 16PLN).

Validate your ticket on boarding by punching it in one of the orange machines near the door and keep it in case of inspection.

MINIBUSES

You will see minibuses zipping about on various main streets around the Planty and particularly from the Old Town down to Podgórze or Kazimierz and out to Wieliczka. These are private enterprises but regulated. The destination is shown on the front and you pay the driver or sometimes there is a conductor. Fares vary but are roughly double those on official city buses. Most begin at the main railway station. They can seem a bit daunting to non-Polish-speaking visitors but many tourists use them.

TAXIS

Use only metered taxis, which are clearly marked. Charges are moderate, like most things in Krakow. There are handy taxi ranks just within the Planty at Plac Szczepański, ul. Sienna and ul. Sławkowska, and also at the junction of ul. Stradomska and ul. Bernardyńska. To call for a taxi, try Radio Taxi Wawel on 12 266 6666 or 19666 from your cell; Mega Taxi on 12 400 0000 or 19625; Nova Taxi on 12 633 9444 or 19669; or Barbakan Taxi on 19661 or at www.barbakan.krakow.pl (website has English version). Certain fleets will offer a 10 percent reduction for those who book by telephone.

VISITORS WITH DISABILITIES

Krakow is above all a wonderfully well-preserved medieval city and many premises are prevented by their historic nature from installing as many facilities for visitors with disabilities as they might like. Since the mid-1990s Poland has required all new public buildings to have wheelchair access. This law also applies to the refurbishment of older buildings. The city restoration schedule means many but not yet all of Krakow's museums now have ramps and elevators.

Contact the Galeria Stanczyk information center for visitors with disabilities (ul. Królewska 94, tel 12 636 8584, open Tue, Thu 11–5).

OFFBEAT TOURS

● Insiders Creative Tours by car or on foot offer their own perspective on Essential Krakow, Criminal Krakow, Women of Krakow and the completely wacky Night Taxi—a hilarious and intriguing tour led by "Professor Vodka." From 70PLN per person ☎ 12 421 4835, www.krakow-tours.info.

● Communism Tours by Crazy Guides take you around Nowa Huta in a Soviet-era Trabant or out to an old-fashioned farm for dinner. From 119PLN per person ☎ 500 091 200, www.crazyguides.com

CITY CYCLING

As a flat city with many students, Krakow is full of cyclists, bike rental firms and bike tours.

● Cool Tour Company city bikes, tandems, recumbent bikes, penny farthings, cost from 6PLN an hour. Also bike tours by day and night from ✉ Courtyard, ul. Grodzka 2 ☎ 12 430 2034, www.cooltour company.com

● Cruising Krakow city and country tours cost from 75PLN and bike rentals from 15PLN for three hours ✉ ul. Basztowa 17 ☎ 12 265 81057, 514 556 017, www.cruisingkrakow.com

Essential Facts

ELECTRICITY

● In common with the rest of Europe, Poland has a 220-volt electrical system and uses round-pin plugs.

MONEY

The złoty is the official currency in Poland, usually abbreviated to zł. or PLN. There are 100 groszy (gr.) in one złoty. Banknotes come in denominations of 10, 20, 50, 100 and 200 złotych; coins as 1 złoty, 2 złote and 5 złotych, 50, 20, 10, 5 groszy, 2 grosze and 1 grosz.

LOST PROPERTY

Try the local government Biuro Rzeczy Znalezionych at ul. Wielicka 28, office 114, tel 12 616 5713. For lost property on public transportation, tel 12 254 1150.

MEDICAL TREATMENT

For minor ailments, try a pharmacy (*apteka*) first. Many speak English.

● For 24-hour medical information, tel 12 661 2240

● For 24-hour private medical services, try Scanmed, tel 12 629 8800; or Medicover, tel 500 900 500

● For ambulance service, tel 999 or 112 (general emergency number) from a cellphone

MONEY

Bank cards are widely accepted and there are many cashpoint machines (ATMs), especially in the main tourist areas, with several in the Rynek Główny and in the main streets of the Old Town. Compare the bank rate of exchange with that of one of the many foreign exchange bureaux *(kantor)* before changing your money—you may find a better rate. Do not change money with anyone in the street. On entering the European Union, Poland pledged to adopt the euro but no date has been set and there is considerable internal opposition to it.

OPENING HOURS

Shops choose their own opening hours. In general this is Mon–Fri 10–6 or 7, with earlier closing on Saturday. Within the Planty and around Kazimierz shops are often open on Sunday too. Grocery and food shops open earlier and stay open later. There are many small 24-hour supermarkets in the Old Town, especially on the inner edge of the Planty. Even beyond the Planty, convenience stores stay open 7am–11pm or midnight. Most museums are closed on Mondays. Banks are generally open Mon–Fri 8–5, Sat 8–1.

POST

Some of the assistants at the main post office speak English (Poczta Główna, ul. Westerplatte 20, Mon–Fri 7.30am–8.30pm, Sat 8–2). The post office near the railway station has some round-the-clock services (ul. Lubicz 4, open 24 hours for letters, faxes, courier services, otherwise Mon–Fri 7am–8pm). You can also buy stamps at kiosks. Postboxes are red with a symbol of a yellow horn in a blue disc and the legend Poczta Polska.

PUBLIC HOLIDAYS

● 1 Jan (New Year's Day)
● 1 May (Labor Day), 3 May (Constitution Day)
● Ascension Day (40 days after Easter)
● Feast of Corpus Christi (Thursday after Trinity Sunday, which is 60 days after Easter)
● 15 Aug (Feast of the Assumption)
● 1 Nov (All Saints' Day), 11 Nov (Independence Day)
● 25 Dec, 26 Dec (Christmas)

TOILETS

A triangle often designates male toilets *(męski)*; a circle women's *(damski)*. Public toilets and many cafés charge 1PLN to use their facilities.

TOURIST INFORMATION

City Tourist Information Network
www.krakow.pl
● Town Hall Tower, Rynek Główny 1, tel 12 433 7310, open daily 9–7.
● International Airport Krakow-Balice, tel 12 285 5341, open daily 9–7.
● ul. Szpitalna 25, tel 12 432 0110, open daily 9–7.
● ul. św. Jana 2, tel 12 421 7787, open daily 10–6.
● ul. Józefa 7, tel 12 422 0471, open daily 10–5.
● CORT, ul. Powiśle 11, tel 513 099 688, open daily 9-7.
● Wyspiański 2000 Pavilion, pl. Wszystkich Świętych 2, tel 12 616 1886, open daily 9–7.

EMERGENCY NUMBERS

● Police, Fire and Ambulance (general SOS) ☎ 999; from a cellphone ☎ 112
● Police ☎ 997
● Fire *(straż pożarna)* ☎ 998
● Police stations
✉ Rynek Główny 29 ☎ 12 615 7317
✉ ul. Szeroka 35 ☎ 12 615 7711
● Polish Tourist Organization emergency number Jun–Sep 10–10: from a landline ☎ 0800 200 300; from a cellphone ☎ 0608 599 999

EMBASSIES AND CONSULATES

● **British Honorary Consulate** ✉ ul. św. Anny 9 ☎ 12 421 7030, www.gov.uk ⏰ Mon–Fri 9–3
● **Consulate General of the United States of America** ✉ ul. Stolarska 9 ☎ 12 424 5100, www.krakow.usconsulate.gov ⏰ Mon–Fri 8.30–3
● **The Embassy of Canada in Warsaw** ✉ ul. Jana Matejki 1/5 ☎ 22 584 3100, www.poland.gc.ca ⏰ Mon–Fri 8.30–4.30
● **The Embassy of Ireland in Warsaw** ✉ ul. Mysia 5 ☎ 22 849 6633, www.embassyofireland.pl ⏰ Mon–Fri 9–1, 2–5

Language

In Polish every letter is pronounced and the stress is almost always on the penultimate syllable. Ą is a nasal "on," while ę is also nasal. Say i as in the English "me." The vowel y is gutteral as in "myth;" j provides the English y sound as in "yeah;" ó and u are as in the English "cool." Cross English l and w sounds to get ł. The letter c is like ts in "bits;" g is as in "get;" r is rolled; ń is a softer n with a "ye" aftertaste and ź is like the French j in "journal." Certain pairs of letters are said as one sound: ch, like the Polish h, is hard as in the Scottish "loch;" cz is like English ch in "church;" ś and sz like English sh as in "shed;" rz as Polish ż, like English s in "leisure."

USEFUL WORDS

yes	tak
no	nie
please	proszę
thank you	dziękuję
you're welcome	proszę bardzo
excuse me/I'm sorry	przepraszam
where?	gdzie?
here	tu, tutaj
there	tam
when?	kiedy?
now	teraz
later	później
why?	dlaczego?
who?	kto?
May I? Can I…?	Czy mogę…?
good morning/ good afternoon	dzień dobry
good evening	dobry wieczór
good night	dobranoc
hello	witam
goodbye	do widzenia/do zobaczenia
bye	zobaczenia
hi	cześć
left/on the left	po lewej/na lewo
right/on the right	po prawej/na prawo
open	otwarty/czynny (shops)
closed	zamknięty/nieczynny (shops)
today	dzisiaj/dziś
tomorrow	jutro

DAYS OF THE WEEK

Monday	poniedzialek
Tuesday	wtorek
Wednesday	środa
Thursday	czwartek
Friday	piątek
Saturday	sobota
Sunday	niedziela

MONTHS

January	styczeń
February	luty
March	marzec
Apri	kwiecień
May	maj
June	czerwiec
July	lipiec
August	sierpień
September	wrzesień
October	październik
November	listopad
December	grudzień

SEASONS

Spring	wiosna
Summer	lato
Autumn	jesień
Winter	zima

EMERGENCIES

Help!	*Pomocy!*
Stop, thief!	*Łapać złodzieja*
Can you help me, please?	*Proszę o pomoc?*
Call the police	*Proszę zawołać policję*
Call an ambulance	*Proszę zadzwonić po pogotowie*
I have lost my wallet	*Zgubiłem portmonetką*
I have lost my passport	*Zgubiłem paszporta*
Where is the police station?	*Gdzie jest komisariat policji?*
Where is the hospital?	*Gdzie jest szpital?*
I don't feel well	*Źle się czuję*
first aid	*pierwsza pomoc*

NUMBERS

1	*jeden*
2	*dwa/dwie*
3	*trzy*
4	*cztery*
5	*pięć*
6	*sześć*
7	*siedem*
8	*osiem*
9	*dziewięć*
10	*dziesięć*
20	*dwadzieścia*
30	*trzydzieści*
40	*czterdzieści*
50	*pięćdziesiąt*
100	*sto*
1,000	*tysiąc*

USEFUL PHRASES

How are you? (formal)	*Jak się pan/pani miewa?*
Very well, thanks	*Bardzo dobrze, dziękuję*
How are you? (informal)	*Jak sie masz?*
I'm fine	*Ja jestem wspaniałe*
I do not understand	*Nie rozumiem*
How much is it?	*Ile to kosztuje?*
Do you have a room?	*Czy pan/pani ma pokój?*
How much per night?	*Ile kosztuje za dobę?* (doba means a night and a day)
with bath/shower	*z łazienką/z przysznicem*
When is breakfast served?	*Która godzina jest śniadanie?*
Where is the train/bus station?	*Gdzie dworzec/dworzec autobusowy?*
Where are we?	*Gdzie jesteśmy?*
Do I have to get off here?	*Czy to mój przystanek?*
I'm looking for…	*Szukam…*
Where can I buy…?	*Gdzie można kupić…?*
A table for… please	*Proszę stolik dla…*
The bill, please?	*Rachunek, proszę?*
We didn't have this	*Nie jedliśmy to*
Where are the toilets?	*Gdzie są toalety?*

Timeline

Given the many border changes and reversals in their country's history, resilient Poles are apt to make jokes as to whether Poland is a place, an idea or simply a state of mind.

CULTURED CAPITAL

Between the 11th and 17th centuries Krakow was the capital of Poland but even when the country disappeared entirely under the partitions of the 18th and 19th centuries the city remained an artistic and intellectual powerhouse as part of the province of Galicia, which stretched in a crescent east from Krakow through to present-day Ukraine.

Władysław Jagiełło statue (left); Józef Piłsudski, Polish soldier and statesman (middle); Poles fleeing their country in 1939 (right)

c.50,000 BC Evidence of settlers on Wawel Hill.

7th–8th century AD Era of legendary founder King Krak and his daughter Wanda.

965 First written record of Krakow by Ibrahim ibn Jacub, a merchant from Cordoba.

c. 1038 Kazimierz I (the Restorer) declares Krakow capital of Poland.

1257 Krakow city charter granted by Duke Bolesław the Chaste.

1364 Krakow Academy, forerunner of the Jagiellonian University, founded by Kazimierz III the Great.

1386 Child bride Queen Jadwiga of Poland marries Grand Duke Władysław Jagiełło, Grand Duke of Lithuania, joining the two countries.

1596 King Zygmunt III moves Polish court from Krakow to Warsaw.

1655–57 First invasion of Krakow by Swedish forces.

1772 First of three partitions of Poland between Austria, Prussia and Russia. Krakow under Austrian occupation.

1793 Krakow under Russian occupation after second partition.

1795 Krakow part of Austria after third Polish partition. The country of Poland ceases to exist.

1850 Great Fire of Krakow razes half the city.

1918 Poland regains independence after 123 years of foreign occupation.

1939 Nazis occupy Krakow on 6 September.

1941 Krakow's Jews evicted from their homes and taken to the new ghetto at Podgórze.

1943 Liquidation of the Podgórze ghetto.

1945 Red Army enters Krakow.

1949 Construction of the Socialist-Realist district of Nowa Huta begins.

1978 Krakow put on Unesco World Heritage List; Cardinal Karol Wojtyła, Archbishop of Krakow, elected Pope John Paul II.

1990 Solidarity leader Lech Wałęsa elected President of Poland after fall of Communism.

2004 Poland joins European Union.

2007 Krakow celebrates its 750th anniversary.

2015 Poland marks 70 years since the liberation of Auschwitz.

QUEEN, KING, SAINT

Queen Jadwiga was all three. As a girl, she rejected her lover in favor of a marriage that would be politically advantageous for the country she was to rule. One of two queens of Poland who was also crowned king, she was canonized by Pope John Paul II at a Mass on Błonia Fields in 1997.

CROWNED HEADS

Even after the capital moved to Warsaw, the kings of Poland continued to be crowned at Krakow's Wawel Cathedral. The crypt is still the resting place of Poland's heroes to this day.

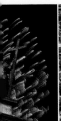

Zygmunt's Column (left); Lech Wałęsa, the trade union activist and politician (middle); Pope John Paul II (right)

Index

Krakow 25 Best

WRITTEN BY Renata Rubnikowicz
UPDATED BY Marc di Duca
SERIES EDITOR Clare Ashton
COVER DESIGN Chie Ushio, Yuko Inagaki
DESIGN WORK Tracey Butler
IMAGE RETOUCHING AND REPRO Jacqueline Street-Elkayam

Published in the United Kingdom by AA Publishing

ISBN 978-1-1018-7944-3

FIRST EDITION

All details in this book are based on information supplied to us at press time. Always confirm information when it matters, especially if you're making a detour to visit a specific place. Fodor's expressly disclaims any liability, loss, or risk, personal or otherwise, that is incurred as a consequence of the use of any of the contents of this book.

SPECIAL SALES
This book is available for special discounts for bulk purchases for sales promotions or premiums. For more information, email specialmarkets@randomhouse.com.

Color separation by AA Digital Department
Printed and bound by Leo Paper Products, China

10 9 8 7 6 5 4 3 2 1

A05314
Mapping data supplied by Global Mapping, Brackley, UK © Global Mapping
Transport map © Communicarta Ltd, UK

The Automobile Association would like to thank the following photographers, companies and picture libraries for their assistance in the preparation of this book.

Front cover: From left to right: Pawel Kazmierczak / Shutterstock; Morganka | Dreamstime.com; Pawel Kazmierczak / Shutterstock; Pawel Kazmierczak / Shutterstock; S-F / Shutterstock; Deymos.HR / Shutterstock

2–18t AA/Anna Mockford & Nick Bonetti; 4–6 AA/Anna Mockford & Nick Bonetti; 7cl AA/Anna Mockford & Nick Bonetti; 7cc AA/Anna Mockford & Nick Bonetti; 7cr Czartoryski Palace museum; 7bl AA/Anna Mockford & Nick Bonetti; 7bc AA/ Anna Mockford & Nick Bonetti; 7br AA/Anna Mockford & Nick Bonetti; 10–14 AA/ Anna Mockford & Nick Bonetti; 15bl AA/James Tims; 15br AA/Anna Mockford & Nick Bonetti; 16–17 AA/Anna Mockford & Nick Bonetti; 18tr Max Jourdan; 18tcr AA/Anna Mockford & Nick Bonetti; 18cr AA/Anna Mockford & Nick Bonetti; 18bcr AA/Anna Mockford & Nick Bonetti; 18br AA/Anna Mockford & Nick Bonetti; 19i Marilynne Lanng; 19ii–vi AA/Anna Mockford & Nick Bonetti; 20–30 AA/Anna Mockford & Nick Bonetti; 31 Marilynne Lanng; 32–39 AA/Anna Mockford & Nick Bonetti; 42t Jagiellonian University Museum; 42c AA/Anna Mockford & Nick Bonetti; 42–43 Marilynne Lanng; 43tr AA/Anna Mockford & Nick Bonetti; 44–45 AA/Anna Mockford & Nick Bonetti; 46tl Czartoryski Palace museum; 46c Czartoryski Palace museum; 46–47 AA/Anna Mockford & Nick Bonetti; 46cr AA/Anna Mockford & Nick Bonetti; 47–59 AA/Anna Mockford & Nick Bonetti; 62tl AA/Anna Mockford & Nick Bonetti; 62tr AA/Anna Mockford & Nick Bonetti; 62–63 AA/ Anna Mockford & Nick Bonetti; 63tl Marilynne Lanng; 63tr AA/Anna Mockford & Nick Bonetti; 63cr AA/Anna Mockford & Nick Bonetti; 64–69 AA/Anna Mockford & Nick Bonetti; 72–85 AA/Anna Mockford & Nick Bonetti; 88–90 AA/Anna Mockford & Nick Bonetti; 91 National Museum in Krakow; 92–96 AA/Anna Mockford & Nick Bonetti; 97 AA/James Tims; 100–103 AA/James Tims; 104 AA/A Mockford & N Bonetti; 105 AA/James Tims; 106t AA/Anna Mockford & Nick Bonetti; 106c AA/James Tims; 107 Hotel Copernicus; 108–112t AA/Anna Mockford & Nick Bonetti; 108tr AA/ Anna Mockford & Nick Bonetti; 108tcr Hotel Copernicus; 108bcr AA/Anna Mockford & Nick Bonetti; 108br AA/Anna Mockford & Nick Bonetti; 113 AA/Anna Mockford & Nick Bonetti; 114–125t AA/Anna Mockford & Nick Bonetti; 124bl AA/Anna Mockford & Nick Bonetti; 124bc Hulton Archive/Getty Images; 124br Keystone/ Getty Images; 125 Polish National Tourist Office

Every effort has been made to trace the copyright holders, and we apologise in advance for any unintentional omissions or errors. We would be pleased to apply any corrections in a following edition of this publication.

Titles in the Series

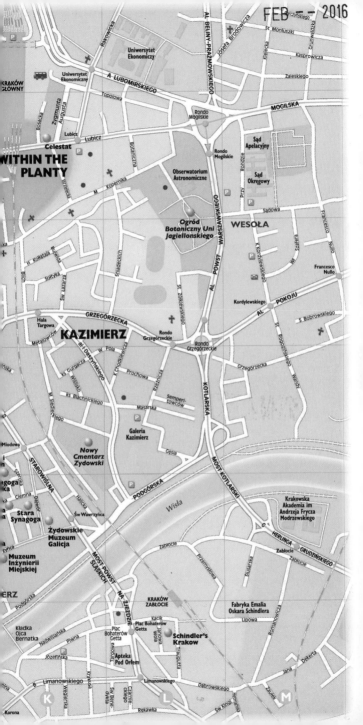